# PRAISE FOR
# NAVIGATING THE UNKNOWN

"This book should be gently placed in the hand of every woman or man who has found out their baby is not alive or will not live long. Amie Lands thoughtfully covers every question that races through the mind of a parent dealing with unfathomable grief. I only wish this book had been available when I was faced with the questions and topics she addresses. Grandparents, friends, birth workers and anyone who loves someone facing the devastating loss of a child would be well-served to read this book."

—LAURA MALCOLM, Co-Founder, *Give InKind*

*"Navigating the Unknown* is a book that all parents should have access to when navigating the death of their baby. This practical guide is a light during times of darkness. Amie does a beautiful job exposing the unknowns, which drastically decreases the anxiety that accompanies these situations. I only wish I had this book when my son died."

—KILEY HANISH, OTD, OTR/L, Founder, *Return to Zero Center for Healing*

"This is the book I wish was available when grieving our own very personal loss. Amie so beautifully and tactfully guides readers on how to navigate life after loss. Her words not only help the reader feel less alone with their emotions but offer compassionate support and concrete resources to seek healing as well."

—BERYL AYN YOUNG, Founder, *Recapture Self and Illuminate E-course*

"As a bereaved mother and passionate advocate for grievers, *Navigating the Unknown* is a must-read for any parent facing a future without their baby. It offers much needed insights and practical advice on a topic poorly understood and even less talked about. Amie writes from her heart and experience to lead the way for other parents with honesty, compassion, and hope. I've often said there is no manual to guide us through the death of our child—but now there is! Thank you, Amie, for creating this invaluable resource."

—RACHEL TENPENNY CRAWFORD, Co-founder,
*Teamotions*, Founder, *Heal by Choice Cruise Retreats*, and
Certified Grief Recovery Specialist®

"While I chose to write memoir and fiction as ways to process and understand the story of my daughter's life and death, Amie Lands has produced a practical handbook of steps to take, from responding to the diagnosis, to how to "re-enter the real world." She will hold your hand like a dear friend as you wade through the challenges of living on after your baby dies. *Navigating the Unknown* acknowledges the full range of hard emotions you might experience, while calmly and firmly guiding you through."

—DR. MARIANNE ROGOFF, Author, *Silvie's Life and
Love Is Blind in One Eye: 7 Stories*

# NAVIGATING
# THE
# UNKNOWN

Navigating the Unknown is published by Kat Biggie Press.

Kat Biggie Press
http://katbiggiepress.com

Cover design by Michelle Fairbanks, Fresh Design
Book design by Alexa Bigwarfe, Write | Publish | Sell
Editing by Bridgett Harris, Triple B Writing Services
Author photograph by Nicole Sullivan, Nicole Lee Photography

ISBN-13: 978-0-9861969-9-7
Library of Congress Control Number: 2017932611

First Edition: January 2017

10 9 8 7 6 5 4 3 2 1

# NAVIGATING
# THE
# UNKNOWN

*an immediate guide when experiencing*

*the loss of your baby*

## Amie Lands

*My sweetest Ruthie Lou, you gave me the greatest gift — the gift of you. You made me a mama. You taught me true, unconditional love. You showed me beauty in life and in the next place. I live for you. I love for you. I love, love, love you. And, I miss you every day.*

*To those who are in the midst of this journey, experiencing the loss of your child now, I am so sorry you're here. I wrote this book, with all the love in my heart for you and in honor of your precious baby.*

# CONTENTS

# ACKNOWLEDGMENTS

With sincerest gratitude to the doctors, nurses, social workers and support staff at Kaiser Foundation Hospital-Santa Rosa, Kaiser Foundation Hospital-Oakland and George Mark Children's House in San Leandro, CA. Your guidance and support through each step, before, during and after Ruthie Lou, has been instrumental to our healing. Words cannot express how you changed the trajectory of our life in surviving this grief. Thank you.

To those who have walked before me, who showed me I could survive this, thank you. I didn't believe it and I don't know how I got here, but I have not only survived, I am living the life of love that my daughter would wish for me and one I know we all deserve.

To our family and friends who supported us from afar while we lived our life away with Ruthie Lou. We were able to do so because we knew our pets, home and work were tended to and cared for. You allowed us the gift of being present with our daughter.

To our family and friends who continued to support us in our darkest time after Ruthie Lou died. Thank you for standing by us and holding our hearts, while gracefully loving us through it. You may not have known the "right thing" to say, but you showed up anyway. You were our ray of hope that the beauty of our daughter's life would remain, far after her death.

To my husband Chris, my partner and best friend. We did it. We're doing it. We have survived this together. We are living life together. I am so grateful for you and for your beautiful, kind, patient and loving heart. You are an amazing dad. Your love for our three children knows no bounds. I continue to be in awe of you.

To my beautiful boys, Reid and Adam. May you always know that I love you more than anything in the whole wide world and because of your sister, I have become a far better mother. She taught me to love with abandon and I love you both fiercely.

To the team that made this book possible, I am endlessly grateful. Alexa Bigwarfe, Write, Publish, Sell; Bridgett Harris, Triple B Writing Services, LLC; Michelle Fairbanks, Fresh Design; Chido Samantha, Nancy Cavillones; and Nicole Sullivan, Nicole Lee Photography; your contributions made this book far more beautiful than I ever imagined. Thank you for your unending support, and in doing so, supporting an entire community of bereaved parents.

# FOREWORD

*"When it comes to sorrow, no one is immune.*
*It happens to everyone, in one way or another,*
*sooner or later...the loss of a loved one,*
*heartbreak." Alice Hoffman*

The journey of traveling from grief-struck to a place of regained balance, and even grace, is not one for which many of us are prepared, nor one on which we embark willingly. The initial shock of an unanticipated loss can leave us reeling. Mourning the death of someone we love, whether that someone is an infant or a much loved person at the end of a longer life, means grieving the loss of dreams, possibility, and a very special relationship.

In her lovely small, and wise, book, <u>Survival Lessons</u>, Alice Hoffman shares the reason she wrote the book: "All the while I was grieving, I was looking for a guide book. I needed help in my new situation. I needed to know how people survived trauma." Similarly, from the depths of her own mourning, Amie Lands has written a powerful guidebook for helping parents wend their way through the anguish of a child's death. Her book is full of heartfelt, and practical, suggestions to assist readers in navigating the journey of grief and to help them arrive safely and greatly healed. I have been honored to share the walk with Amie and her husband Chris from their heartbreak and devastation to a safe place that includes a new home, bounding with the energy of Ruthie Lou's two younger brothers. Together, Amie and Chris have supported each other's grieving process, and have demonstrated that even in the darkest hour, roses still bloom and the stars still come out at night.

I know that Amie's book has been written with great care and tenderness, to share a message of hope, survival, and healing. May you, each reader, benefit from her willingness to impart her hard-earned wisdom.

DR. KATHY N. HULL
Founder - *George Mark Children's House*

# PREFACE

Dear Parent,

My heart breaks that you are reading this book because it means that you have recently been told your child will, or has, died. From the depths of my soul, I am so incredibly sorry. There are no words adequate to describe the pain of this news; the loss that you feel to the core of your being, in the blood that rushes through your veins, or how every part of your body vibrates with emptiness without your baby in your life or in your arms to hold. The English language does not carry words that can explain this emotion, so for lack of better words to offer, I am so incredibly sorry.

My daughter lived 33 days; we did not know she would die when she was born. We found out a few weeks after that she would never come home. The final days of her life and time surrounding her death live in my mind in an alternate universe, one that I can access without even a moment's notice. I call her life a "time out of time"; the world continued to spin on its axis, people continued their daily routines, but our life stood still, in between life and death.

When you are pregnant, expectant mothers are often gifted the book *What to Expect When You're Expecting,* which later turns into *What to Expect the First Year* and so on, but those resources no longer applied to me. I now needed *What to Expect When Your Baby Has Died.* I needed to know that I could survive her death—that others had survived the death of their child and gone on to live joy-filled lives—as unbelievable as that seemed at the time and often is still unbelievable today. I needed to know what was to come in the days ahead, in the weeks, months and years in my future, and how to overcome the logistical pieces of life when your baby dies. When we were given our daughter's diagnosis and prognosis, we were not provided any of those resources. I could not find written material on how to survive without my child. I looked at every bookstore, I scoured the library, and I searched online to no avail. Nothing was exactly what I was looking for.

The book that you are now holding is what I needed. This handbook is written from my heart and now it can also be your handbook. It covers everything that was relevant to my experience and the experiences of many other mothers I have met and befriended in this "baby loss" community of bereaved parents. All of our experiences have the same outcome, but the stories are each as special and unique as our babies and our love for them. Because our time with our babies varies so widely, I have appealed to those whose baby died before birth, as well as those who knew (or didn't know) their baby's life would be brief. With that said, there are some parts of this book that may not apply to you. Feel free to skip them. I hope that you understand that these parts of the book aren't here to cause more pain, but to include, help and assist as many bereaved parents as possible. That is what we are here for—to hold each other up in our darkest hours of need.

As with the story of our baby's life, our families and life situations vary greatly as well. For ease and fluidity, choices have been made as to how I will be referring to gender and parents in this book. Because this is the book that *I* was searching to find, I will be writing this book to me, as a mom. And since my loss was my beloved daughter, I will be referring to the baby in the feminine. Neither of these choices were made lightly, nor were they intended to exclude a partner, dad or your precious baby boy. However, doing so will help the flow of the reading by maintaining the roles throughout the book.

As you move through this book, know that although you are lonely in your particular walk of grief and loss, you are not alone. There are scores of moms and dads who have also had to say goodbye to their precious child and we all wish we could take this pain from you. I am with you in spirit, holding your hand, holding your broken heart close to mine and sending you all my love on this devastating journey. You can do this, as devastated as you feel, your love can bring you through.

Before you go any further, I must say to you—you will always be your child's mother. You will always be her parent, you will always carry her in your heart and in everything you do for the rest of your life. You didn't fail her, you did the best by her, you loved her, will always love her and long for her. You wanted her, you grew her, you carried her, you birthed her, you held her, you made milk for her, and you did everything right for her. You are an amazing mom. You will always be your child's mom.

ALWAYS.

With all my love,

Amie Lands, forever Ruthie Lou's mama

# INTRODUCTION

This was not supposed to be my life. This was not supposed to be your life. When imagining your future family, I know that you did not imagine your child dying. Yet, here we sit in this club that nobody wants to be part of.

So, use this handbook as it is intended—for support, love and compassion from one bereaved parent to another, who, like you, did not and still does not want to be here. Take what applies to your family and leave the rest. Some sections will connect with you and others may not, but they are all here for you should you be looking for ways in which other families have survived along this road of grief.

**I am not an expert, nor do I claim to be.** I am an expert on my own journey and all of which has led me here. I have lived the chapters that I am writing and the parts that I didn't experience, I have written from the knowledge of other bereaved parents who are experts in their specific bereavement journey. I write from my heart and I write to YOUR heart. These suggestions and ideas are merely things that we have learned along the way. There is no judgement here. There is no right or wrong in anything you decide in your child's life or after her death.

There are many ways that you have arrived here, and even though our journey to this destination is unique, the outcome is the same—your child is dying or has died.

There is no comparing or judgment in grief; we have all endured unimaginable decisions, experiences and loss. Our job is to now support one another and believe that we all did the very best we could with the information that we had at that time, even if now knowing differently, our decisions would be different. Try your best to not judge anyone, especially yourself. Most of us have never walked these steps before and we are doing the very best that we can for our child, for our family, and for ourselves.

This handbook begins for parents who have learned that their child has a life-limiting prognosis or, as doctors often say, is "incompatible with life". Those heavy words come with a variety of horrifying decisions that all need to be made simultaneously while one's child is alive, either in the womb or already born and in the NICU. It is a terrifying time that carries its own set of stress. If these first chapters don't apply to you, skip ahead to the chapters that do. You do not need to read this book in succession but rather use each section as it applies to you.

This is a lonely path, and even though you now have found others walking beside you, it is your journey to take. Any time you feel alone, come back and read the words of this book. Revisit when you need to be reminded that you are doing, have done and did everything right for your child. And know, always, this community of bereaved parents is here to support you, even if we have never met.

# ONE

## Receiving a Life-Limiting Prognosis

IF YOUR BABY HAS RECEIVED a life-limiting prognosis or terminal diagnosis, whether in your belly or shortly after birth, this section is written for you.

Nobody expects to find themselves in this situation. You may have just had an ultrasound, you may have just given birth to your beautiful baby, but instead of hearing exciting news, you were given a devastating diagnosis and/or prognosis. There are difficult decisions to be made or maybe there is no decision at all, but for now you wait. And your family is waiting, too. They may be sitting by the phone or relentlessly checking social media for the update on your baby, they may even be in the waiting room. It can be an overwhelming task to continuously update your family and friends of the most current status—as much as you may want them to be informed, it can be such a time consuming and emotional task to take on.

First, you do not have to inform anyone of anything that you are not comfortable with! You have just received horrifying news and you do not owe anyone anything. It takes such emotional work to process all that you're encountering right now that your sole priority is your health and maintaining the health of your baby.

On the other hand, the people in your life love and want the best for you. While it may seem awkward or uncomfortable to share such intimate details with others, you may find that you want their support, well wishes or prayers in a time that is really scary and overwhelming.

Sometimes, their notes of love can be the bright moments in otherwise dark and dreary days.

Whatever you decide, as with every choice regarding your precious baby, there is no right or wrong. Everything you decide is right for you and you alone. You are the only person that you need to be concerned about. This is your life and your family's experience. You get to choose and know what is right at this moment.

## Ways to Inform Your Loved Ones & Support Sites

**Point Person:** There are many different ways that you can inform your family without having to expose yourself to the time of relaying information individually. The simplest way is to have one point person to inform others of health updates. This person may be a family member or close friend with whom you would already be sharing information. They, with your permission, will pass on the information to your chosen audience whether it be your intimate social circle or your complete social network. A few things to consider when appointing this person:

- Do you trust them?
- Will they represent your wishes as you would like them to?
- Are they self-sufficient in completing the task or will it create more work for you?

It's important that you wholeheartedly trust this person because they will be sharing extremely sensitive information with the world about you and your precious child. Make sure that they have your best interest at heart, that no part of this is for their own benefit or attention. It may sound harsh to say, but in times of great stress, sometimes people can change and do things that are not in your best interest.

**Social Media:** Most people maintain relationships through social media these days, whether it is Facebook, Twitter, Instagram or a personal blog. A simple way to make announcements is to continue with the same platform that you currently use in your everyday life, whatever form that might be. On Facebook, you can create a separate page specifically focused on health updates or you can use your personal page to post status updates as you normally would, if that's how you typically communicate with your friends and family.

**Patient Websites:** There are several webpages created specifically with the intent of sharing health updates. Websites such as CaringBridge, CarePages and MyLifeLine (and more) are offered for free or at minimal cost to create a webpage that can be updated to notify friends and family of your baby's health status. These pages are already formatted for you, to take away some of the stress of needing to be computer savvy. They have done all the hard work and they walk you through creating a personal page to share with your friends. You can choose to be the sole moderator for the page or have others, maybe your partner or a close friend, contribute as well. After creating the page, the link can be shared on your social media. There is also an option for friends or family to be notified (usually through text or email) each time that you update your information. This option can be a convenient one if you choose not to have a point person, but still want updates to be spread far and wide, particularly in your own words and on your own time. Oftentimes, there is space for your loved ones to send you messages and notes of support, as well.

**Crowdfunding Sites:** Loved ones want to help in moments of crisis. Most people hear that someone they love is suffering and the first thing they want to do is lessen your pain. You are probably being asked 100 times, "What can I do to help?" and often, even *we* don't know what we need in the immediate moment of such chaos. But, depending on your situation, some items are needed immediately, such as money. Even with the best of insurance, many families don't have savings prepared for unexpected tragedy. When you find yourself unable to work and/or living in a hospital, there are many expenses that arrive, such as gas to and from the doctor or hospital, parking meters, three meals and snacks a day, hotel stays and daily necessities that we often take for granted. And, if you don't have stellar insurance, hospital bills start mounting the moment you receive your diagnosis and can be upwards of tens of thousands to nearly a million dollars if not fully covered. Crowd Funding sites such as GoFundMe, YouCaring, and GiveForward offer fundraising websites that can be specifically geared to your needs. They allow you to explain your financial needs, your health situation, post updates and information all while encouraging your social group to support you in the only tangible way that they can right now, through easing the weight of financial strain.

Some things to be wary of and questions to ask when researching the best site to utilize:

- What/How are the fees assessed?
- How can a person pay to donate: PayPal, credit card, bank account number?
- How do I access my funds?
- When can I access the funds raised for my family?
- Can I access funds intermittently or only when fundraising period ends?

These sites also allow another person to manage the campaign for you, with the money going toward your cause. Be cautious when allowing someone to handle your money, and choose that person wisely. The last thing you want is to worry about your funds, or your friendship, during this time!

**Support Sites:** Give InKind is an alternative to traditional crowdfunding/patient sites, but is a way to help your social circle navigate this unknown time with you by finding the most thoughtful ways to be supportive. Just as you have never walked this path before, most likely your loved ones have not either and as much as they want to support you, they may not know where to start. Give InKind helps to guide others during any time of need. Although the site is not specific to the death of your baby, it does include resources for you, written by other bereaved parents. Give InKind is filled with articles, information, gifts, and services and is available to help offer resources to those who want to support you and your family, but may need help knowing where to start

# Preparing for Baby

If your baby received a life-limiting prognosis or terminal diagnosis while in utero, you may find that the questions are never-ending. Among them, many families wonder what is normal or what other families have done when they faced such a heart-wrenching prognosis. The first thing to remember is that right now, your baby is still here. Your baby is alive in your belly and with each movement you experience, your baby is feeling the love that you are so freely expressing. Your baby is important, valued and loved and (even though your heart is breaking) it will always be that way.

There are many ways that families honor their baby and you get to be the deciding factor in how you will spend your time while your baby is with you, even in utero. You may or may not have answers to the really scary questions regarding the life of your baby, but here are some things that you can do to celebrate the life that is still living inside of you:

**Create memories with baby:**

- Take maternity photos
- Go on a trip
- See a sports game
- Go to the zoo
- Visit the ocean
- Write baby's name in the sand
- If near a holiday, include baby (stocking, pumpkin, thanksgiving candle)

**Buy special items:**

- Outfit
- Stuffed animal
- Frame for ultrasound pic

**Have a Celebration of Life baby shower:**

- Invite guests to write letters to baby
- Collage affirmations/focus cards for strength during hospital stay
- Bring sacred beads to string together for labor & delivery

There is no "wrong" during this time. Your emotions are most likely going to change day to day, moment to moment. Sometimes you might feel the strength to do the suggestions listed above, other days you might only have the strength to take a shower, or not even get out of bed! All of those things are perfectly acceptable and normal and in no way demean the love you have for your baby. Whether you do something or nothing (external) at all to honor your baby, your love is enough. Your courage to face each day with this prognosis is enough. And for the days when you are sheer out of courage, that is enough too.

# Perinatal Hospice

When you learn that your baby has a life-limiting prognosis or terminal diagnosis, whether in utero or shortly after birth, perinatal hospice is a model of compassionate care provided to you, your baby and your family. A tremendous amount of research has occurred to ensure that families like yours are offered tangible support while waiting to welcome, and ultimately say goodbye to, your baby. Although not a curative approach, the intention of perinatal hospice is to focus on comfort care and the quality of your baby's life. Regardless of the length of time your baby is with you, she is still entitled to a life of love, dignity, respect and grace.

With the guidance of your caregiver, a care plan will be created specific to your family's needs. They will offer you practical guidance, as well as emotional/educational support that begins at the time of discovery in pregnancy and continues through your child's birth, life and the time after, when she is no longer living. The plan that you create with your team will ensure this will happen with the best of intentions.

If you have not been offered or introduced to this practice at your current doctor or hospital, be sure to inquire as to which hospitals in your area can support you. At the time of this publishing, not every hospital has a formalized perinatal hospice program. However, if no program exists locally, your doctor has access to resources and information that can be an integrated part of your prenatal care plan. You deserve this support and you shouldn't have to walk this path alone.

# TWO

## Taking Care of You While Your Baby is in the Hospital

I CANNOT STRESS ENOUGH, how important it is to take care of yourself while your baby is in the hospital. The health of you and your partner is top priority. Your baby has the best doctors, nurses and specialists there to provide round the clock care and while it's hard to let go of the control of your child, you cannot be your best self if you are worn down or ill.

**Meals & Food:** The last thing you may feel like doing is eating and maybe the last thing your body will allow you is sleep, but that is the only way to fuel yourself in this stressful time. Healthy food, ample fluids and quality sleep are your energy sources. You will not be of service or an advocate for your child if you fall ill, become hospitalized or become contagious and cannot enter the hospital room!

How do you fuel yourself while your baby is in the hospital? Lots of planning and lots of help. Your nurses or social worker should be able to provide you with a list of local resources for restaurants, grocery stores, gas stations and hotels in the area. If for some reason, this is not available, then your smartphone, tablet or laptop will be your best friend! By Googling the city that you are in, you should have access to all the local spots that you will need. Local restaurants and hotels may offer discounted prices for patient families and it is important to become familiar with the local area because at this point, you may or may not know how much time your child will be in the hospital.

Grocery stores will be a great place to stock up on snacks that you can have on hand throughout the day. You do not have to be the one to go to the store, you can always send a helpful family member, but you might find that fresh air is a relief after sitting bedside for hours. If you have access to a refrigerator, that is ideal for perishable snacks such as yogurt or hummus. If not, there are plenty of shelf stable healthy snacks available, too. Try to get snacks that will fuel you for the long haul, less simple carbohydrates and more protein or fiber-full snacks that will last throughout the day. If you are a pumping/breastfeeding mama, you will need this fuel to help maintain your milk production, especially while you are in a high stress environment.

**Balanced shelf stable snacks**:

- fruits/dried fruits
- pre-cut veggies
- nuts
- trail mix
- granola bars
- jerky
- pre-mixed protein drinks
- coconut water
- peanut butter
- crackers
- pretzels
- dark chocolate

**Refrigerated snacks**:

- hummus
- cottage cheese
- yogurt
- string cheese
- fresh squeezed (pre-made) juices

Hospital food can be surprisingly appetizing and the cafeteria may be a good place to find your daily meals inside the regular hospital hours. Normally, the cafeteria remains open not only for hospital visitors but also for the workers who have long shifts as well. Make sure to familiarize yourself with the open hours so you do not find yourself starving at a time that the cafe is closed.

If you are tired of hospital food, or the snacks are not holding you over, be sure to choose a healthy restaurant. Look online for local menus or if you found a restaurant without their menu online, you can scour Yelp (sometimes customers will scan the menu) or even call and ask that the manager fax it to the nurse's station. Most places are accommodating as long as it's not their busy time. If you need some fresh air and a change of scenery from the hospital (as many parents do) getting out for a meal is a great escape. Choose a time that is not at the height of the breakfast/lunch/dinner hour. The last thing you want to happen is to be waiting for your food, only to find that you now anxiously want to return to the hospital and you haven't even eaten yet! Many restaurants will also deliver to the hospital, and that is always an option if you don't feel up to leaving.

**Lodging:** There are a few questions you should ask upon meeting your "team" at the hospital. Do they allow parents to sleep in the patient's room? Do they have a family room for sleeping? Is there a local Ronald McDonald house for families? Is there a pediatric palliative care facility available? If you do not live close to your baby's hospital and answers to all those questions are "no," then you will need to utilize local hotels for your lodging.

Your social worker/caseworker/head nurse should know if there are any hotels that offer a discount to patient families. Hotels with late check-out and early check-in are ideal so you do not have to worry about time constraints as you are traveling to and from the hospital. Laundry access will alleviate running out of clean clothes and a continental breakfast will not only save money for that meal but also time.

If the hotel you have reserved does not offer a discount, perhaps sharing your situation will help management locate a different deal that you could qualify for. Hotels are generally big businesses affording them a lot of wiggle room to help their guests. And management are people, too. Everyone wants to feel that they positively contributed to someone in true need and right now, YOU are in true need.

Remember, this is what your crowdfunding money

was intended for. The money that your family and friends have contributed is to lessen the financial burden. It is not limited to hospital bills, but includes all payments that are unforeseen while you and/or your partner are unable to work.

# Pediatric Palliative Care Facilities

If your baby has been diagnosed terminal or with a life-limiting prognosis, but may live beyond pregnancy and birth, you may consider or research if a palliative facility is an option for your family. Pediatric Palliative Care is family centered care that is intended to provide relief from debilitating and painful symptoms for children with life limiting illnesses and those nearing or needing end of life care. Palliative care facilities consist of a team of doctors, nurses, social workers, psychologists and child life specialists whose sole duty is to make certain your child is comfortable and receiving top-notch medical attention in a home-like setting. Not only do they care for the patient medically, your child's team will also tend to your family's emotional needs so that the focus can be providing your baby with love without the worry of handling medical needs.

At the time of publishing (2017), there are only two pediatric palliative care facilities available in the entire continental United States. However, if you happen to be located near one, (George Mark Children's House in San

Leandro, CA or Ryan House in Phoenix, AZ) or if your situation permits you to travel or transfer your child, you may consider using one of these facilities. These houses offer their services at no cost to families, eliminating worry of a future financial burden.

To refer to either George Mark's or Ryan House as "facilities" would not be giving justice to the gift these houses give to their patients and their families. Both of these homes cater to celebrating life with children and their families, for however long or limited that lifespan may be. Upon entering either of these homes, you would never suspect that these are homes for sick children. They are vibrant, lovely and welcoming. Included in these amazing houses are playrooms, playgrounds, warm pools, art rooms, music areas, non-denominational sanctuaries, cafeteria kitchens, children's "hospital" rooms and family suites. Anything that a family might need during their greatest time of pain will be tended to, while their child is being medically supported.

When the time comes that you need grief and bereavement support, these houses both continue their standard of care to include resources for you. Use them. Their love and support for your family does not end with death of your child, they are a resource to continue to guide you through this unfathomable loss. Pediatric palliative care is family centered and care will continue as far in the future as your family may need.

# THREE

## Nearing Final Days, or Your Baby has Died

AT THIS POINT, YOU MAY NOT HAVE NEEDED the previous information. If you have had the devastating experience of your child dying before birth, then there was no need for hotel stays and status updates. There is only one notice—delivering the most awful news you have ever been given to the people you love about the baby that you love more than life. There is no easy way to do this. There is no good way, bad way, better way, or right way to say that your baby has died. There is no timeline, no rush and no reason to do it immediately upon receiving the news or after you have spent time and delivered your baby. Whatever you choose to do during this time is up to you.

As you are learning or have learned, you will deliver your baby or may already have. There are so many decisions to make in the next few days. It can be overwhelming and scary and lonely. Breathe. Although you may feel anxious to move through all these steps or others may be pressuring you to move quickly, it is imperative that you stop and breathe.

It is also important to remember that this is the only time that you will have with your baby. Whatever your reactions and emotions are during this time, even if different from your partner or family, all are perfectly normal. Every person feels grief differently in his or her body; there is no right or wrong. Your body is most likely experiencing shock and that can also add surrealism to the whole experience. There is no rush here. This is the time to slow down and be as present as you can; these are the moments you will never get back. Please greatly consider how you spend this time with your baby and strongly consider creating memories as listed in the section "Memory Making with Your Child." You will not regret any time spent together, but time is one thing that you can never recover.

## How to Deliver the Hard News to Family and Friends

The time that you have with your baby is valuable and it is up to you with whom you choose to share these sacred moments. Making the announcement that your baby has died will introduce an additional dynamic into this sacred time with your partner, your family and your time with baby. When others hear the announcement of your loss, your phone may start to fill with calls, texts and emails and public messages will be posted to your social media—even if you have not shared publicly yet. For some, that will provide comfort and for others, that can create an extra layer of stress. Before doing anything, you will need to ask yourself, what is best for me? Will having text messages, phone calls, social media alerts add to my stress or will they show me that although I walk this alone, I am also comforted in love?

Once you have determined what you would like (announce immediately or share time with your family before moving to a larger announcement), then settle into that decision. Don't second-guess it, don't feel guilty, just allow yourself to be present in the time that you have and in the moments after saying good-bye to your baby. You will not get that time back.

You can always choose to tell select groups of people. You may ask that they keep this information private until you are ready to tell the world, or you may want them to help spread the news, alleviating you of that task. Be clear with what you want and also understand that even with stating your wishes, some may or may not honor them. Be prepared that if you ask for discretion, some may not be emotionally capable of keeping this heartbreaking news to themselves.

**Phone Calls**: You may want to be the one making the phone calls to family and friends, or you may not have the emotional energy to make those calls yourself. It is perfectly acceptable to allow someone you trust—your partner, family member or best friend—the honor of making that call for you. It is an emotionally taxing and draining process to share this news and many will have questions, comments and statements that you may not be ready to hear or answer quite yet. Having someone make the call for you can act as a buffer to any conversation that you are not prepared for.

**Text Messages**: With the luxury of smart phones comes the ability to deliver this hard news through text message, eliminating any need to have a verbal conversation. You can have one general message that you copy and paste to each person or you may have one message prepared that you then ask a trusted person to send on your behalf. Remember, you do not need to respond to any incoming messages as they arrive unless you want to. You may also want to include that note in your outgoing message, that you might need space for a while.

**Social Media:** Social media will inform the largest group of people in the shortest amount of time. The benefit to posting on social media is that in many cases, most people will send condolences through the online platform and your phone may be less affected. The negative is that when you sign on to your site again, all those messages and comments will be there waiting for you. Be prepared for that.

Whatever way that you choose to make this horrifying announcement, know that that is the right choice for your family. Be thoughtful in your words and be clear with what you need in this moment. Some things to consider:

- Do you want to share the cause of death?
- Do you want visitors?
- Do you want to be contacted through texts or phone calls?
- Will you need financial assistance for medical bills/missed work?
- Do you want other bereaved parents referred to you?

- Do you want space to be with your family?
- Is now a good time to start a meal train?

**Explaining to Children:** We always want to protect and shelter our own children (or children that we love) from all pain and hurt in their young lives. However, sometimes we underestimate how much they understand and what they will comprehend. Before making the large announcement, if you have other children or small children in your everyday life, you will want to consider how to deliver this news to them, so that they are not informed from an unexpected person.

Remember when speaking to children (depending on the age of the child) that their understanding of reality is much different than ours. The words and explanation that we give children must differ from that of an adult conversation. It is ok not to have all the right words and not to have all the answers to their many questions. It is equally ok to cry and display emotion in front of children. Children learn from adults and they are learning grief is a natural emotional response to death. It is important for you to be authentic so that they can feel safe to do the same.

Death is very abstract and hard even for adults to understand, so be prepared to answer the same questions over and over again, not only when informing the child but also in the days, months and years to come. As the child matures and ages, your answers and responses will as well. The words you use with a toddler will be much different than those used with a teenager.

Having a professional help you share this news may also alleviate any anxiety about what to say to your child. If you want help sharing this news, ask the hospital if there is a chaplain, social worker or Child Life Specialist that can assist you. They are best trained in these areas and will be able to offer the most carefully chosen words, when your words may fail you. Be sure to meet with them prior to the conversation with children so that you (and the professional) are on the same page as to what and how you want this to be presented. If this support is not an option or one you choose not to use, here are some suggestions:

- Sit close to the child, hold hands or just be near them.
- Be simple in your explanation.
- Use appropriate words such as death and died.
- Be clear, but not scary.
- Use simple words, and concrete examples to explain death.
- Avoid euphemisms such as: lost, born sleeping, passed away.
- Be careful not to say they were sick and died. This explanation can create fear of future illnesses.

- Be direct that baby will not be coming home with you.

- Assure them that this is rare and does not mean that YOU or they will die.

- Be clear that it was nothing that they did to cause this.

- Do not give extra details.

- Ask if they have any questions.

- Answer their questions simply but articulately.

- Name the emotions that they express and reassure them that their feelings are normal and natural.

- Love them and hug them through their tears.

- Allow them to show their emotions; some will not show any emotion at all—that is ok, too.

- Let the child guide the conversation, more will come up as time passes.

# Do We Have Visitors? Who Meets Baby?

The question of whether to have visitors applies whether your baby is critically ill or if your child has died. This practice is not something that our society often discusses, but it is something that regularly happens and it is a sacred experience to be part of. This is the one opportunity that friends and loved ones will have to meet your baby, to hold her should you choose and to adore your child alongside you. This is also such a tender and valuable time with your baby that you do not get to repeat. The choice then becomes, do you spend that time sharing your baby with others or do you keep that time to yourself?

Having visitors meet your baby can be such a beautiful and sacred time to share with loved ones. You may decide that there are people so important in your life that you cannot imagine them *not* meeting your baby. This might be something that is not even a second thought. If so, do it. Call them (or have someone call for you) and tell them how much they mean to you and that you want or need them there. They will feel honored that you feel this way about them. But, with that said, understand that some loved ones may decline. The thought of meeting someone who is dying or has died is not something that our society generally practices and it can be very scary. I hope you will find the space in your heart to understand that if they choose not to meet your baby, it is not a reflection of their love for you or your child, but that their decision is solely personal to them. It also may be a decision that they regret later. But once again, that is for them to consider, not you.

You may also decide that you do not want anyone to meet your baby. If you feel strongly in that decision, then accept it without question. You do not have to share this time or your baby with anybody. You cannot get these moments back and if you and your partner decide you want to savor them for yourself, that is perfectly ok. There is no right or wrong here, there is no entitlement of others to consider. You and your partner are the only people you need to worry about right now.

**Family:** Family carries such an interesting dynamic and no two families are alike. I cannot tell you that you should or should not have family come to meet your baby because that choice is unique to you. This is not a time to act from duty or obligation, this time is precious and should be treated as such. If you are close and comfortable and supported by your family, then you will know the best answer. If your family does not support or comfort you in a way that feels safe, then this is not the time to bridge that gap.

**Friends:** Many times, we find that our friends have become the family that we choose. These friends are the people that you may want to consider having meet your baby. It also doesn't mean that they have to meet baby. Good friends will understand that whatever you have decided in these moments has nothing to do with them personally and everything to do with what you need. Do not feel obligated to do anything you are not 100% certain about. Do not worry about hurting someone's feelings. Your friends will love you through this difficult time, no matter what you decide.

**Children:** We often think that we are protecting our children by not exposing them to the realities of life (and death). Children are very understanding and resilient, many times even more so than their adult counterparts. Remember, the children in your family (whether siblings or cousins) love this baby and they were looking forward to meeting her. Should you choose to have them visit, it can give them a greater understanding of why baby won't be coming home and will help facilitate their healing as well, by creating memories of meeting baby. It is a large choice to make, but it is highly encouraged to allow this to be a part of a child's healing. You will be amazed at how in tune children are to these precious babies, how they see beyond the fear that adults carry and how pure their love is. If you are unsure how to talk to your other children, this time can best be guided by the chaplain, social worker or Child Life Specialist at the hospital. That is their job and they are the experts here.

If you are undecided about sharing your baby with others, here are some questions to consider:

- Will this person be of comfort or cause stress?
- Will this person know the magnitude of this meeting?
- Will this person be able to be present and helpful?
- Will I be comfortable asking them to leave when I am ready to be alone?
- Will this person be able to look beyond death

and see the beauty of my baby?

- Do I trust this person to share time that I cannot again retrieve?
- Will I regret it if I do not include this person?
- Will I regret it if I do and the relationship changes in the future?

# Religious/Spiritual Care Services

You may (or may not) have been offered spiritual care services. Often, one assumes that spiritual care only refers to a religious affiliation and that is not always so. Be up front with your medical team, doctors, nurses and/or social worker on what your family believes culturally and spiritually so that your needs are met for your family and your baby. Rites of passage or sacraments can be tended to in baby's hospital room at any point in time, before or after death. Spiritual leaders or chaplains can be arranged by the hospital, but your family can also call in your personal spiritual advisor as a guest to facilitate, guide or counsel any spiritual and cultural needs that your family practices.

If you are not religiously affiliated but would like additional support, a chaplain may be of great service to you. Chaplains are trained to serve the emotional and spiritual needs of others. They include a multi-faith community and come from a variety of backgrounds. Their intent of practice is in caring for a person's mind, body and spirit. Chaplains offer emotional support by listening to family members in the moment of crisis and can act as an advocate to help meet your family's needs during this very personal and terrifying time.

This time in your life is most likely completely unexpected. Having the support of someone you trust spiritually can help reassure and guide you through. Having another person to walk this journey with you helps to alleviate the isolation you may be feeling. Also, it is very important that your baby be honored in the same way any living child would be, and that includes allowing your family to offer spiritual care in line with your beliefs and customs.

## Memory Making with Your Child

There are many memories that your family can make with your precious child, whether your baby was born living or born still. Some families are uncomfortable with this thought, or think that they do not want to interrupt this valuable time by doing these "arts and crafts". But I caution you, this is the only time that you will have with your baby. The time that you get to hold your child is far less than it ever was supposed to be and once you hand your baby over for the last time, that is it. You don't get that time back, but you can hold those keepsakes for the rest of your life. So, if there is one thing that I am passionate about, it is memory making. It doesn't matter if you think you will or will not want these items in the future, it is better to have them and never use than not have them at all.

Memory making provides not only the tangible gift of the item created, it gives you precious memories of you parenting with your baby. Research has shown that families who have met, bathed, dressed, and spent time with their baby are better able to cope in the healing process; it helps our brains to comprehend what has happened and these activities allow you to parent your child in the only way that you can.[1]

This is a sacred time, holding your child in the space between this life and next—treat it as such. It can be scary, not knowing what to expect. Maybe you have never seen a person after death and the unknown can be overwhelming. But remember, this is your baby. You created this perfect being and she will always be perfect to you. Each moment you choose to spend with her will be treasured for the rest of your life, even if it is the most painful of times. I wholeheartedly encourage you to be present with your child. Be her parent and mother (or father) her as only you can.

---

[1] Institute of Medicine (US) Committee on Palliative and End-of-Life Care for Children and Their Families; Field, M.J., Behrman, R.E., editors. *When Children Die: Improving Palliative and End-of-Life Care for Children and Their Families.* Washington (DC): National Academies Press (US); 2003. APPENDIX E, BEREAVEMENT EXPERIENCES AFTER THE DEATH OF A CHILD

There are many crafts that can be done to commemorate and memorialize your sweet baby, but first, use this time to hold your baby. Feel the weight of her in your arms, smell that baby smell. Unravel that hospital blanket and adore the beautiful baby that you created, that grew in your body. Look at her fingers, toes, the folds of her ear. Find any birthmarks or "angel" kisses, any similarities between baby and mom or dad. Bathe your baby, diaper her, put her in the outfit you had imagined or in the one brought for you. Swaddle her up and offer for your partner to hold baby. Hand baby gently to him/her and notice the look of love in your partner's eyes, even when covered by tears and pain.

**Photos**: Call a photographer, preferably a professional. The nationwide non-profit photography company, Now I Lay Me Down To Sleep (NILMDTS) employs volunteers who are specially trained to photograph families whose child has died or who is dying. They offer this remembrance photography to parents with the free gift of professional portraiture. There are no fees, they are extremely sensitive photographers, and all prints will be edited beautifully and delivered to you. If, for some reason, a photographer is unavailable or you choose not to use one, NILMDTS will digitally retouch any photos you took personally. Having these photos gives you the ability to display your baby in your home or to create a remembrance album to share should you choose to do so.

If you choose not to call NILMDTS or a similar organization (or if you do not have access to a professional photographer) please ask your nurse for access to the hospital camera if you do not have access to one of your own. Most Labor and Delivery units or the nursery down the hall will have a camera on the floor and will allow you to take your own photos. They may even offer to take some pictures for you. If you have family members coming to meet baby, ask them to stop for a memory card on the way to the hospital, that way you can take a surplus of photos. It is better to have more than you think you will want versus wishing you had taken more pictures. This memory card also gives you an opportunity to take photos without having pictures open up every time you use your phone. It also offers privacy to view, edit, enhance, order, or print from them from your home computer when you return home.

It doesn't matter if your child is alive or has already died, photos can be the most powerful memento you have of time with your baby. Although you might decline photos of your child because you do not want to remember her in this state, these photos may be the only pictures that you have of your precious baby. One of the largest regrets of grieving families is the wish they had taken more photos of their child and with their child. Your emotional response to these photos will change as your grief changes and as time passes. As years go by, you may think that you will remember every nook and cranny of your baby, but somehow, the brain forgets even the most delicate of memories. Photos don't allow you to forget, they hold those memories for you. Also, you might find that you want to share your baby with those unable to meet her and photos make that possible. You will be surprised how many people will be open to seeing pictures of your baby.

Be sure to take all the photos as you would any newborn baby. Capture the sweetness of her body; fingers, toes, ears, her little chin, nose, those eyelashes, and any hair on her head. Be sure to get in the pictures with her; you holding her, kissing her, partner holding her and your family together. If any other family members are there, include them, even the children. Leave no photo idea unsnapped. This is your chance to capture every moment of your time with baby. Take advantage of it, for as long as you feel inclined. You may even choose to have the photographer stay for a while, capturing all the small moments that are not posed, including family time.

**Photo Checklist**:

- clothed
- nude
- in diaper
- hands
- fingers
- feet

- toes
- chin
- nose
- lips
- ears
- eyelashes
- hair
- baby bottom
- being held
- in bassinet
- on scale, showing weight
- with special items
- with mom: holding, faces close, kissing, adoring baby
- with dad: holding, faces close, kissing, adoring baby
- with siblings: parent holding baby, siblings adoring baby, individual siblings holding baby
- with grandparents or guests: holding, kissing

And, in all pictures, authentic unexpected emotions are ok.

You will never know the value of these pictures until time has passed. These photos may stay safely tucked away, or you may find that they become treasured memories in the future. They are tangible proof that your child existed in this world. They can be a source of comfort when you need to gaze upon the beautiful baby that you love so much.

When you arrive home, be sure to back up any digital photos that you have taken. CDs have the shortest "shelf life" as far as storage ability, so search for other, more secure avenues. USB flash drives (AKA thumb drives) are small data storage devices that are easy to store, inexpensive to purchase and easy to copy files to. An external hard drive has a large storage capacity, is mobile, is not reliant on any one computer and does not affect the storage space or speed of your computer. Online sharing sources such as Dropbox, iCloud, Carbonite, Photobucket, Google Photos or Amazon Prime Photos can provide safe storage through the internet with access to your photos anytime from anywhere. Each company has its own storage capacity and annual fees if you choose a larger storage size. You have many storage options, you can be the judge of what best suits your needs. Be sure to choose more than one safe place for your photos, because nothing can replace them.

**Arts & Crafts:** When you were pregnant, chances are you dreamed of all the cute arts and crafts you would do with your child: hand and foot prints, paintings using their chunky little feet, newborn photo shoots showcasing every little part of them … I am so sorry you will not have a lifetime of those experiences. There are still many arts and craft activities and items available for you to do while you have time with your baby and it is highly encouraged that you do so. If you have invited family members to visit and meet your child, I would recommend that they pick up this list of items below on the way to the hospital. These things may or may not be used, but you will at least have the option if the items are already with you.

- digital camera memory card (SD Card)
- hand/foot imprint mold
- hand/foot 3-D mold
- tempura paint
- small canvases (for hand/foot prints)
- a large decoupage box (to store items created & cards received)

**Stamps, Imprints, Molds & Keepsakes**: Stamps, imprints, molds and keepsakes offer a tangible memory of your baby to treasure. You may want to put the imprints on display in your home or keep them in a special place to be taken out when you are ready or want to share them.

**Stamps:** Footprints are included in the standard of care for most hospitals. Traditionally, when a child is born, footprints are taken by hospital staff and included in your paperwork upon discharge from the hospital. In your case, it is important that you are certain that this is done for your baby if prints are something that you would like to have. Also, be clear that you want them to take handprints as well; you most likely will treasure these prints. Some parents later use these stamps as the foundation of art projects in their home with pre-existing or future children and some even use them as tattoos. Typically, the stamp is done on special stamp paper so the ink is invisible on your child's skin. If you want more than one stamp or you want it on a special canvas with paint, this would be something to talk about with your nursing staff. Upon returning home, it is extremely important to make a copy of these prints to avoid them from fading in future years.

**Imprints**: Hand and foot imprints are the next step up from a stamped print. Imprints are made from a clay-like substance that will harden over time, giving you a realistic imprint of your child's hands and fingers, their tiny feet and sweet little toes. This is moderately gentle for baby skin and can later be painted or sealed with spray paint to help it last over time.

**Molds:** 3-D molds are actual 3-D replicas that are created by sticking your child's hand and/or foot into the mold using a kit purchased from a craft store. The 3-D mold is amazing in its authenticity to your child's actual hand and foot. You can see every nook, cranny, fingerprint and hand-line. You can hold their actual foot in the palm of you hand when they are no longer with you. This process is less delicate and will not do well if your child died before birth. You will have to be the judge, along with your nurses, to know if using a 3-D mold is appropriate for your baby. Also, 3-D molds are a bit temperamental to create. I would definitely ask a nurse or family member to assist you and your partner and I would certainly purchase more than one kit, should it take the first try to practice the procedure. When you return home, similar to the imprints, be sure to seal or paint the molds so that they survive the elements that could erode or fade them over time. A sealing spray paint will be sufficient to seal the porous material of the mold.

**Keepsakes**: Many families want to gather the keepsakes from their child to put in a baby book, a special box or chest. Among these items, families have chosen to include hospital bracelets, locks of hair, or other memorabilia. For some, the thought of cutting your baby's lovely locks (should they have hair) may not be ideal, so be sure to ask the nursing staff to do so for you. While you are in the hospital, please be sure to care and store these items safely by putting them in a special place until you can find a permanent spot in your home. You won't regret making these mementos and someday may find yourself longing for them if you don't have them.

## What to Expect in Your Child's Last Moments & in the Moments After

If your child is born living, there will come the time that their body starts to shut down. Nothing can emotionally prepare you for this. It is ok for you to question what to do; it is ok to not know what you want. It is ok to want to run, while at the same time never wanting to leave. Breathe. Remain present. Follow your heart. Listen to that little voice in your head that reminds you that you are your baby's parent and you will do anything for her. This is that time. Push away the fears that you have and remember the love. Be present to give all your love to your child.

**The Dying Process**: Please, please, please ask your medical team to explain to you and your family what to expect in your child's last moments alive. Being equipped with information can lessen the fear of the unknown in this dying process. Each scenario is unique and, therefore, is beyond what I can predict for you. Your doctor and nursing staff should be able to be specific regarding your child's situation.

What I can tell you is that like birth, death can be a very spiritual experience. It is also devastating, soul crushing and heartbreaking. But like birth, as parents, we parent our child in all the good and the bad, the joy and the hurt. This will be one of the hardest things you will ever have to do, but you can do it. Your love for your precious child will give you the strength to be with her and bear witness to this transition.

If your child has already died and you are reading this after the fact, know that however her death occurred, you did the best you could with what you had in that moment. You did all the right things, even if you now have regrets. There are always regrets, this is normal, no matter the circumstance.

**In the Moments After**: You may not have been witness to your child's death, whether it happened out of your sight or while your baby was in utero, but it is very normal to not know how to respond after your baby has died. Some want to run away as fast as they can to escape the pain of loss and some never want to leave their baby, knowing these are the last moments. There is no rush. Nothing else in the world matters right now. You do not need to make an immediate announcement about your child dying. You will have plenty of time to tend to the world later.

You may be encouraged to spend time with your baby after she has died. This sacred time can be for as long or as little as you want (if there are no organ donations to be made), but you will want to have the process explained to you. Be clear in asking questions and expressing your wishes to your medical staff. Allow them to alert others to give you the space you request of them. Some hospitals have what is called a Cuddle Cot. This machine will help regulate your baby's body temperature so that the effects of dying will be slower, thus allowing more time with your child. If your hospital does not yet have a Cuddle Cot, please ask how they can best support the time you have with your baby.

Your medical team will ask you if you want to hold

your baby. Say yes. It may feel scary, but you will never regret doing this. This is the beginning of a series of things that you never thought you would do, never thought you would be capable of doing and obviously would never want to do. But this is your baby, the one you love and will forever love and these are your last moments. Now of course, there is no judgement if you are unable to do these things or if circumstances prevented you from being able to do them. These recommendations are for you, from others (including me) who want to save you from feeling regret later. You don't know what you will regret or wish that you had done during this time, so say yes to it all. Listen to the doctor, nurse, or social worker you trust most and say YES.

Here are some suggestions for the time after your child has died:

- Breathe
- Stay present
- Trust your instincts
- Follow your heart
- Light a candle
- Talk to your baby
- Sing to baby
- Read baby a children's book
- Pray or give blessings over baby's body
- Play music
- Bathe your baby

- Adore baby's naked body, booty, toes, fingers, ears, chin, cheeks
- Dress baby in her finest outfit
- Take LOTS of photos (refer to previous section, *Photo Checklist*)
- Swaddle baby
- Hold baby as long as you want, there is no rush

**Cuddle Cot:** The devastating reality after your baby has died is that the dying process continues after the moment of death and your baby's body will start to decline. A Cuddle Cot is a cooling device that is inconspicuously hidden in a Moses basket or something similar. The cooling allows the natural progression of death to occur more slowly. This creates additional time to be with baby, and allowing you to spend as much time with your child as you feel comfortable. Having that time also allows for other children, family members or supportive friends to meet baby if that is something you choose to do.

Not every hospital has a Cuddle Cot, but it is worth asking. If for some reason they do not, and you wish to have additional time with baby, there are other ways that your nursing staff can help to keep baby's body at a cooler temperature. Please speak with your nurses so that they are clear about your desires and to discuss your options. Your nurses are the biggest advocates for your family, communicating clearly with them will create vital support.

**Handing Your Baby Over**: At some point, you will decide, along with your medical staff, that it is time to say your final goodbye and hand your child over for the last time. Be part of this decision; do not feel forced to hand your baby over if you are not ready yet. The last moments that you have with your child are ones you will always remember. You can choose to make this goodbye quick or create a ritual type setting. Your child knows you love her. Chances are, you will be handing your baby off to someone you may not know, or have only known briefly in your child's life. My hope for you is that they realize the magnitude of this moment and treat it as the sacred event that it is. When the moment has come and you have said goodbye, after baby has left the room, know that I am hugging your broken heart.

# FOUR

After Your Child Has Died

**A NOTE ON MEMORY MAKING:** If you have skipped the previous chapters because they did not apply to you, because your baby died before birth or you did not receive this handbook earlier, I urge you to read the section on memory making as it applies whether your child was born living or not. This time with your baby is sacred and the mementos created will be treasured items when you return home and in the years to come.

## Decisions: Autopsy, Organ Donation, Burial Gowns, Arrangements

I am so sorry that you have to make these unthinkable decisions. I wish that it weren't so. Hopefully, until this point in your life, you have not needed the information that will follow. Unfortunately, this is information that you need to know now and these are decisions that you will need to make.

**Autopsy:** If you were given a diagnosis while your baby was in utero, you may not have or feel the need for an autopsy. But, if your baby was stillborn or died unexpectedly, you may consider asking for an autopsy. Don't assume that one will be offered; it may not be. It also may not be covered by your health insurance, so be prepared for that.

An autopsy will most likely be done in a matter of days, with results being returned about 6-8 weeks after the procedure. Having an autopsy will not negatively affect the timeline of a funeral, nor will it be evident that an autopsy was performed if you choose to have a viewing. Pathologists who perform autopsies are very respectful in this process, knowing and understanding that your baby is precious and loved. Although this is a clinical procedure, they will take care in tending to your child.

In the autopsy results, you may not receive any answer as to why your baby died. Unfortunately, even with an autopsy, many families are not given an answer as to how or why their baby has died. In addition to an autopsy, you can also request that baby's placenta be examined and that genetic testing take place. Sometimes answers can be found in these procedures, but be prepared for many unanswered questions.

When you do receive the results, they will be filled with medical information regarding your baby that may be difficult to read. If you feel unable to read the results yourself, ask your doctor to help decipher the results or bring them to a genetic counselor or personal counselor who can best explain the contents in a safe and supportive environment. You may not want to read the results and that is fine, too. Some families have needed/wanted to bring these results when considering future pregnancies, so just be sure to keep them in a safe place should you need them for medical reasons.

**Organ Donation:** Organ donation may not be offered to you, it may be something you feel strongly attached to, it may be something your religion is opposed to or it may be something you never considered for yourself, let alone your precious baby. Should you want to investigate organ donation as an option, asking the doctor, nurse or social worker is the best place to start. They will connect you with a representative from the National Registry to help answer any questions you may have. Organ donation can save the life of, or add significant value to the life of, another baby. Unfortunately, not all babies are appropriate for organ donation. If donation is important to you, then that would be the first question to ask your medical team. Organ donation is very detailed and specific in what can be donated and the manner in which this process unfolds. It is important to ask any questions that come to mind and to do your research, if time allows. For some families, organ donation is simply not an option due to the cause or timing of death.

Many families who choose organ donation do so in the hope that good comes from their baby's short life. It brings them comfort knowing that another life is improved or saved, even when their own baby could not be. Whether you choose donation; want donation, but it is not possible; or choose against donation, you are doing the best thing for your baby, your family and your heart.

**Burial Gown/Outfit:** Every family chooses something different when leaving their baby for the last time. There are options, should you choose to adorn your baby in a traditional burial gown. Many non-profits create gorgeous pieces for both boys and girls to be buried or cremated in. Ask your hospital if they have a relationship with any local seamstresses or if they happen to carry burial gowns in the hospital, as many do. If for some reason your hospital does not, a burial gown can truly be anything that you want it to be. Some parents want their baby to be dressed in her most beautiful piece of clothing, some in the outfit that baby would have gone home in, and some want their baby nude but swaddled in a blanket. Some moms have made the shopping trip for their baby as a sacred experience to choose the last outfit their baby will wear. Others are not attached to a burial gown at all and instead prefer to use something that they planned for baby before they died, something they always imagined them to be clothed in, had they lived.

The main consideration in choosing a burial gown or outfit is to remember that you will not get this piece of clothing returned. While that may seem logical, some parents have expressed wanting to memorialize the item of clothing. If you think that might be the case, perhaps choose something that you can purchase in two identical pieces, one for baby to wear and one for you to keep.

**Burial/Cremation:** After your child has died, you will have to make so many heavy decisions, including whether to cremate or bury your child. I am so sorry that you have to make these choices. Ask your hospital if there is a social worker who can help guide you if you are not certain about one versus the other. A social worker has been trained in this area and can help to gently support you during these unfathomable choices. Many times, couples have not made these decisions for themselves, let alone considered what they would want for their beloved child. If you have a cultural or religious belief that supports cremation or burial, chances are the decision is already made for you. In the case that you do not have a religious affiliation or are unsure, most families imagine what they would want for themselves when they die, and then make that decision for their child as well.

Some questions to consider:

- Do I want a place in which to "visit" my child on special or lonely days?
- Do I want my child's name in print for others to know of her existence?
- Do I want a gathering place for family members to honor my child?
- Do I want to spread my child's ashes to return to the Earth?
- Do I want my child close in my home, on my mantel or an altar?
- Do I want to create memorial items or jewelry from her ashes?

Also, remember that many of these wishes can be fulfilled regardless of burial or cremation. Memorial jewelry can be created using symbols or pictures and ashes can be buried to have a "gathering place" and headstone that many families desire. If you are unsure, take your time. This decision is lifelong. Sleep on it and try to make the choice that leaves the most peace in your heart.

**Funeral Home/Mortuary:** When searching for the funeral home or mortuary that you will use, inquire if the hospital has a reference list or a relationship with any local facilities. Many (but not all) funeral homes or mortuaries will discount their services, as they realize how unprepared families are to afford these services for their infant. Also, if the hospital has a pre-existing relationship with a facility, it may make the transition from hospital care to after-death decision-making slightly less painful, as mortuaries are trained in this particular type of loss.

Although at first glance it doesn't seem that the funeral home and mortuary are much different from one another, there are a few minor differences that you may want to consider before making the decision about which one to use. Essentially, the purpose of both is to prepare your baby's body for the burial or cremation service. The other support or services you are looking for will determine which type facility that you select.

**Funeral Homes:** Funeral homes are more of a full-service facility with a funeral director who can help to facilitate many facets of the after-death arrangements. They have services available to support you, as they have experience in planning. Sometimes they even offer grief counseling or referrals to others in your community. One thing that funeral homes likely do not have is on site cremation services, but they will make the transportation arrangements for cremation (or to the gravesite in the case of a burial), so that is not something you will need to worry about.

**Mortuaries:** Mortuaries are less inclusive, but are typically less expensive. They do not normally have a funeral director and are more focused on the actual after death arrangements. Their dedication and quality of work are equal to those of a funeral home, but with less emotional support than you might find at a funeral home. That said, they do typically have on-site cremation services in which you would be able to be present for the cremation if that is important to you.

**Home Funeral:** Some families opt to bring their baby home to prepare her for either burial or cremation. The Funeral Consumers Alliance claims that: "all but eight [of the United] states allow the family to complete the entire funeral process by themselves without hiring a funeral home." There are legal restrictions or requirements in many states, but you as a parent are able to spend valuable and precious time with your baby before you must proceed with after death arrangements. One benefit of a home funeral is financial (as home funerals cost next to nothing). Also, being at home gives you more time with your baby than if you chose a mortuary or a funeral.

Many families want to bring their baby home to the place they had envisioned their future to be. As part of a home funeral, you are the director and deciding person. There are many non-profits available to advise you and they often have an advocate to help guide you through the process.

Some questions you might want to ask yourself when deciding between a funeral home, mortuary or home funeral:

- Do I want the support of a funeral director?
- Are finances a factor in this decision?
- Do I want support for planning a service?
- Is on-site cremation important?
- Will my family want to view baby before cremation/burial?
- Will my family want to be present at the cremation?
- How comfortable am I with handling my child and the death services on my own?

## Honoring Your Baby's Life, Obituary, Announcement

Your baby's life is valuable. You get to choose the best way in which to honor her. You may want the world to witness the honoring of your beautiful baby, want only those sacred to you to be present or only want it to be you and your partner and living children (if you have other children). You may also decide not to hold a ritualistic event and that is fine, too.

The way in which you honor your baby will never equate to the love you have. There simply is no celebration or ritual that could possibly encompass such a thing, nor can it express the amount of pain and sadness that their loss in your life has brought. But, you can do your best and know that whatever you plan for your baby (even if that means abstaining from this ritual) is the best way for you to express your love for them.

Funerals, Memorials and Celebrations of Life all have similar aspects. Each of these services honors your baby and encourages the gathering of loved ones to support one another. It is an opportunity to share your baby with those who may not have met or known her, and all ceremonies are intended to be healing rituals.

Here are some examples of what other bereaved families have done in honor of their baby:

**Funeral:** Funerals have been in existence for centuries, their history being well defined in religious or cultural ceremonies. They traditionally consist of three parts: a vigil/viewing, a funeral service and a burial/graveside service. The body of the deceased is usually present. Funerals are planned in conjunction with a religious leader (depending on what affiliation you have) and are traditionally held in a religious building with some sort of reception after. Funerals typically have a religious leader speak on behalf of the family; there may be poems, scripture, song and other speakers, and sometimes the stage is left open for community members to speak about their love for your baby. Families with strong cultural or religious beliefs traditionally choose to hold a funeral for their baby, as that is what they would choose for themselves.

**Celebration of Life:** Celebrations of Life are not usually religious, although the ritual manner of a having a service to honor a loved one is similar. These services traditionally allow family members the freedom to be more creative and are usually more focused on celebrating the life your baby had, even if she lived only in your womb. Families may tell stories of their baby, sing songs, read written works and have a reception after. These can be held indoors or outdoors, and while they may be very spiritual (or not at all) they are usually not religious. Because this type of event is not directed by any affiliation, family members have the freedom to organize the type of event that feels most comfortable to them, including or eliminating any parts that they want.

**Memorial:** Memorials are the middle ground between funerals and life celebrations, as they can be religious or non-denominational. As opposed to funerals, a memorial does not have the body present for viewing. Since there will not be a viewing as part of this service, families have more time for planning and/or processing before holding the actual event. The actual event may mirror a funeral with a set program that is followed, allowing space for the family to add their own personal additions to a day that is really intimate for them. A memorial may still have a burial or graveside service that is generally private or mainly for family members. A reception is typical for grievers to gather and support one another.

**Planning:** There are many parts to consider when planning this event. This may be one of the only times that you plan an event for your child and although you never envisioned having to plan a funeral, memorial or celebration of life for your baby, you get the honor of presenting her precious life to the world. Remember to consider all aspects of planning and know that there are other people wanting to help you. This is a tangible opportunity for people to support you. Let them.

Here are some important questions to consider:

- Who will you invite or want to have in attendance?
- What type of service will you hold?
- Where will you hold the service?
- Will you be involved in the writing of the eulogy?
- Will you want to speak or sing at the service?
- Will you hold a reception after the service?
- When is the location available that works in your timeline?

- How will you afford this event?
- How will others help support you in creating the event that you envision?
- How will you announce the service?
- Will you add an obituary to the local newspaper?
- Are there community members who can help donate items, venues, services or food to the event?

In addition to the type of service a family chooses, there are many ways to creatively make your child's service unique. Here are some ideas that bereaved families have created:

- Mom and/or Dad speak about baby's life and the impact she had and will always have
- Invite family members to speak
- Show a slideshow of photos for others to "get to know" and/or "meet" baby
- Create a written program
- Design a memorial bookmark or magnet
- Have a trinket to take home, a symbol for others to remember baby by
- Release sky lanterns, balloons, butterflies, ladybugs
- Have food, snacks, a meal or potluck
- Invite those closest to them to visit their

home after the larger event has ended to decompress

**Obituary:** Many families have found that writing their baby's obituary provides a keepsake to have for future years and tangible proof for the community that their child existed. Although it can provoke many feelings to write about your baby for an obituary, it is also a great way to alert a large number of people about the sacredness of your child's life. This is an opportunity to guide the community that surrounds you on how you would like to be supported and how you want your baby to be remembered. You can also announce any services, inform community members how to honor your baby and request how to best contribute to your family's healing. This obituary can run for one day, or as long as you choose. Also, many newspapers offer an online version allowing visitors to leave messages to your family that may be of comfort for you to read and reflect on later. Some families consider re-running the obituary for their child annually, to honor and commemorate their baby's life, and reminding others to keep speaking their child's name.

**Announcements:** When a family arrives home with their living baby, it is customary to send out a birth announcement celebrating the new life. Some families still choose to do this with their baby, even if they were not born living or if their life was short-lived. There are companies that will create unique birth/death announcements, but any stationary store can accommodate this request and many stationary websites are available online, should you not want to visit a specialty store. An announcement may invite others to acknowledge your baby and give them the courage, permission and the ability to approach you about your baby if they were previously unsure of how to proceed. These cards are beautiful and can be modified to include exactly what your family wants to share and will also set the tone for how you want your baby to be remembered. You can choose to include a photo, your baby's hand or footprints or a special symbol that honors your baby. Typically, an announcement would include baby's name, important date(s), measurements including weight & length, and anything else you want your friends and family members to know about your child. This card can be a treasured keepsake, not only for you, but for the recipients who love and miss your baby as well.

# FIVE

## Being Home

# Body Changes: Lactation Support, Ceasing Lactation, Milk Donation

THERE ARE SO MANY EXTERNAL THINGS TO TEND to during this time, with so many decisions to be made and emotional stresses weighing on you. You also just delivered a baby and your body needs to recover. The physical changes that have occurred to your body since giving birth need attention. It is important to listen to what it needs and tend to your body as needed. Your emotional healing will take much longer than the few weeks that your body needs, so please be gentle with yourself and make certain to give your body its much-needed rest to recover

**Lactation Support:** Unfortunately, your body will not know that your child has died and chances are you will begin to produce milk. Every woman's body is different, but you can expect that your milk will come in within the first days after delivery. The amount of milk production is unique to each individual and it may seem to be a cruel joke that you did not have the choice that your child died, but now you have to make a choice in how to proceed with milk production.

You do have options and you do have help. You can stop lactation or you can continue by pumping and choose to donate your milk. Some moms find healing in giving milk to another mother's baby in the NICU. Some moms find that they can heal better without the engorgement of their breasts. Only you will know what is best for you. Do not feel pressured to choose one way or the other.

It is important to take care of yourself during this time, no matter what you decide. Eating enough and drinking ample fluids are important to your breast health regardless of your decision. Improper care (and even proper care) can sometimes lead to a breast infection. If you notice any adverse reactions while ceasing or encouraging lactation, such as pain, fever, swelling, tender red spots or sores, contact your physician right away, as these could be signs of mastitis.

**Ceasing Lactation:** Some moms choose to stop milk production. A doctor, nurse and/or lactation consultant can help guide you through this process, which can take several days, even up to a week or more. You may notice that your breasts become engorged with milk, which can be quite painful. Here are some ideas to manage pain as you reduce your milk supply:

- Avoid allowing warmth near your breasts. This may prove difficult in the shower or bath; turn your back to avoid the warm water or take a bath while in a seated position.

- Wear a fitted sports bra to create a "binding" effect on your breasts.

- Insert ice packs in the bra or even cold cabbage leaves. The idea is that if warmth creates milk stimulation and leakage, the cold will help to alleviate that sensation. Your local drugstore may carry flexible ice packs and some stores even have them in breast-specific shapes for easing sore breasts.

- If you find engorgement is occurring, hand express or pump only long enough to relieve the pressure and build up. Do not express beyond the relief, as that will confuse your body into creating more milk. Moist warmth, such as a shower or wet washcloth, can help soften the breast to release milk.

- Ibuprofen can be taken for pain (check with a medical professional).

- Drink ample amounts of fluids to remain hydrated while your body is working to heal itself.

**Donating Milk & Encouraging Milk Production:** Some moms choose to continue milk production to donate their breast milk. Breast milk is then donated to milk banks. In this case, you will pump (or continue to pump) breast milk on a regular basis and follow the guidelines set forth by the various milk banks in your local area. Each bank has its own guidelines and requirements, and you will need to be approved as a donor. Be certain to contact them for details before storing ample amounts of milk. After being approved as a milk donor, you will create your own schedule of pumping to encourage your body to continue to produce milk. Here are some tips for successful pumping:

- Relax, breathe, be present.

- Stay hydrated. This is referred to as "priming the pump." Make sure you have a glass of water nearby when you sit down to pump, too.

- Have a regular pumping schedule. Just as with breastfeeding, stimulating your breasts alerts your body to create milk. The more you stimulate milk production, the more your body will create for you.

- Pump when you wake in the morning. Milk production is usually at its highest upon waking; you may find most success at this hour.

- Think of your baby. Hold a picture of your baby, if you have one. Sometimes the visualization of your baby can assist with "let down".

- Alternatively, do not think of your baby. This contradicts the point made prior, but for some moms, being reminded of your baby as you pump can bring up the stress related to your grief and this can inhibit milk production.

- Store your milk in the appropriate bags or containers as needed by your chosen milk bank and be sure to label them immediately. Store your milk in a deep freezer or in the back of your kitchen freezer.

# Healing from Birth: Postnatal Care

You may not remember to take care of yourself in the days after returning home without your baby. Be gentle with yourself; you have just delivered a baby! Regardless of the external stress that you may be experiencing, it is really important that you tend to your physical healing and recovery.

- For both vaginal and caesarian recoveries, you can expect soreness, bleeding and contractions, all of which are normal. Your body is healing from a major experience and/or surgery.

- Healing times vary from person to person, but can take up to and beyond 6-8 weeks. Be patient and gentle with yourself regardless of the speed at which you recover.

- To alleviate painful symptoms, use your doctor-prescribed medicine and/or over-the-counter pain medication as directed. If pain is extreme, inform your doctor.

- Use the hospital-issued peri bottle filled with

warm water after each trip to the bathroom. Not only will this feel relieving, it will also help keep your genitals cleansed and free of bacteria.

- Resume movement as soon as you are comfortably able. This will improve circulation and bowel function.

- No sex, tampons or douche until your 6-week checkup and when approved by the doctor.

- Invest in comfortable yet large/long pads; you may have bleeding and lochia discharge for several weeks.

- Request to be given stool softeners and gas relieving medicine before being discharged from the hospital. They are good to have on hand in case you need them.

- Kegel exercises can begin as soon as you are ready. These will strengthen all the muscles that have been stretched and overworked not only from delivery, but also from the pressure of carrying extra weight on your pelvic region.

- Rest. Rest is so important; allow your body the strength and energy to heal your physical wounds.

Here are some other tips and reminders for healing from delivery.

**Vaginal Delivery**:

- If it is painful to sit, a "donut" or "waffle" type inflatable device can offer some relief while you heal.

- A sitz bath (a bath in which only the buttocks and hips are immersed in water) can reduce pain and swelling. Fill your tub with a few inches warm water, rest gently in tub making sure genitals are fully soaking. Do not use any products in the water. Pat dry when done.

- Use a peri bottle to spray your genitals if you have pain while urinating.

- To ease pain and soreness, soak a maxi-pad in witch hazel. Chill the witch hazel for an even greater coolness.

- Moist wipes are useful to reduce the pressure from wiping sore areas; don't "wipe" but instead press lightly to clean yourself.

**Caesarian Delivery**:

- For the first weeks, driving and stair walking are discouraged; check with your doctor for the go-ahead.

- Do not lift any heavy items. Ask for help from your partner for any heavy lifting.

- Take gentle care of your incision area. Avoid any obvious elastic, jean buttons or tight fitting clothes during your healing time. Purchase large, high-waisted underwear to avoid chafing of elastic on your incision.

- Take warm showers using only mild soap and allow the water to run over the incision area, being careful not to scrub. Avoid baths until your incision is healed.

- Use a "binder", a pillow or your hands to help maintain pressure on your incision when raising to stand or lowering to sit, as well as when coughing, laughing, or sneezing.

- Use a C-section salve on your incision once it is closed. The salve will eliminate itching during the healing process.

## Home Support: Meal Trains, Groceries, Housekeeping, Childcare

**A Note on Home Support:** Your loved ones want to help you, but they don't often know how. Please refer to section two regarding support site, Give InKind. There, you will be guided by those who have experienced this loss, ways in which your social network can help, comfort and support you during your transition home, including the following suggestions.

The first few weeks at home are a whirlwind. You may (or may not) be planning a service for your child, you will be making after death arrangements for your child, all while healing from recently giving birth. This is the time to reach out to all the people who love you and want to offer support. Now there is actually something tangible for them to do. This is when you need your tribe!

None of the suggested help below needs to happen while you are at home or is an excuse for people to come into your space, if you are not ready to share space with them. All of this help can be arranged through a friend, family member or business, and you can relieve yourself from any obligation of interacting with anyone until you are ready.

**Meal Trains:** You may find when you return home that you do not want to do anything from your old life, including shopping or cooking. A unique way for your circle of support to help tend to you is to participate in a meal train. This can be done in a variety of ways: manually with phone calls and a point person to coordinate the calendar, or through online websites.

Websites offer a seamless system on how to coordinate a meal train, complete with meal ideas and information on how to deliver pre-made meals. Many times, families who are unable to offer a meal will prefer to help with the grocery shopping or a gift card for a restaurant that delivers. Those are great options for busy families who want to help but may not necessarily have the time (or skill) to contribute in this way.

**Groceries:** Even though you may not feel like eating, you need to fuel your body with nourishing food to help recover from delivery. Grocery shopping at your neighborhood store can be an overwhelming task, as you will be surrounded with people who have not seen you since before your child died. To try and avoid this (if you are not ready) you can opt to shop in a neighboring city where you can be anonymous. Try online grocery shopping if that is available in your area or make a grocery list for a friend who is willing to shop for you. The goal is to get groceries in your house, it does not matter the manner in which that happens. Allow others to take care of you, or use a service that will allow you to take care of yourself.

**Housekeeping:** Your housecleaning will not do itself. Even if you are not "getting dressed" each day, yoga pants and t-shirts still need to get washed and the dirty clothes will still pile up. If you have other children, you know your house is being destroyed daily. Housecleaning help can be a tremendous relief as the dust settles (no pun intended) and you may need an extra hand with daily chores.

Having someone help clean the house is not necessarily an invitation to socialize. You get to decide if you are present during the scheduled cleaning time. If you choose to stay home, you are entitled to lock yourself in your room for privacy or you may find that the helping hand opens the line of communication while you work side-by-side. It is all up to you.

You may prefer that a paid housekeeping company does the cleaning so that you don't feel obligated to converse. You also might find that having a friend or family member to help lend a hand may feel more comforting to you. Be sure to communicate your preference when setting up help or speaking with the coordinating friend, so that there isn't an opportunity for confusion or hurt feelings later.

**Childcare:** Having living children at home does not allow you, a grieving parent, the time it takes to tend to your broken heart. While you may feel like lying in bed all day with the curtains drawn, your little (or big) ones at home still require that you tend to them as well. Childcare is a beautiful gift to give grieving families. Not only are the parents hurting, but their other children just experienced the loss of their brother or sister as well. Siblings also have to navigate a world of grief that is difficult even for adults!

It is important that childcare is done with a person who can be sensitive to the children's needs and will understand and be patient with perhaps otherwise ill behavior. We all "act out" when processing unknown feelings, and children are no different. This can be a time that you may see a different side to your child and it is important that whoever you choose to spend time with your little ones can be sensitive to that.

Childcare can be a creative outlet for your kids to express themselves with someone other than you. They may already sense your grief. Keeping kids at home may allow them to feel like their territory is still "safe," but having another pair of eyes on them can allow you the space that you need to take a much needed break from your parental duties.

You can opt for your childcare helper to come over while you are at home and be a helpful hand if you just need another adult to shoulder the responsibilities of parenting with you. You could also take this time to get out of the house (if the kids will be staying) and be outside, in nature, at the mall or treating yourself to some self-care—a massage or acupuncture. If you decide for your helper to take the kids out of the house, this is a rare opportunity to lay in bed, journal, soak in a warm tub, watch a TV show or movie, or do anything that you cannot comfortably do with your children around. Whether you use this time to process your grief emotionally, exercise it out physically or zone it out with some distractions, all are important and necessary parts of taking care of you! Take advantage of this time and do whatever your heart needs at the moment, even if that means you cry the entire time your kids are occupied. Crying is so important.

# Emotional Support: Online Resources, Local Resources, Counseling, Retreats

Grief is all encompassing. As a society, we are not well prepared to handle grief or to know what to expect. Having a support person or a support group may help to reassure you that you are not alone and that your responses to your grief are normal. It may seem that you will never recover from this loss, and for a long time that will feel true. Although your life will never be the same (your innocence lost and your heart forever longing for your baby), you can survive this. Recovering will not be easy, it will not come without feeling the hard feelings, but there are avenues that can help to heal your broken heart.

Finding emotional support after your baby has died is crucial to your healing, recovery, health and well-being. Often, parents find support in the comfort of other bereaved parents, those who have experienced a similar loss. There are numerous places to find emotional support, whether it is online, local or with the help of a trusted professional. The avenue in which you pursue this is less important than the fact that you actually receive support. Grief is an isolating experience, but the support of others helps to alleviate the loneliness.

**Online Resources:** With the advancement and availability of the Internet, there are so many resources for support online. However, with the enormity of information available, it is important to know which are the "safe" and supportive websites to visit.

When searching for an online resource for support, you want to look at the content being provided and the manner in which information is being presented. There are many blogs and websites available that share personal stories of other bereaved families, but not all pages are created equal or with a healthy intention. It is easy to get lost in other stories. These stories may be of comfort to you for some time, but be sure to look for the pages that offer you hope. Hope will be your lifeline in these early days of grief.

Social media pages offer many public and private groups that you can join to create community. If you want to maintain privacy, you may consider joining a private group so that others in your life cannot view your conversations. There are also many public groups that you may find strength in participating, even with the knowledge that other people in your life can see (and hopefully support) what you are experiencing.

*Still Standing Magazine* is an online magazine, created in 2012 after the death of the founder's beloved daughter. This online site is a way for parents to connect by reading articles written from the bereaved perspective, with all articles written by families impacted by infant or childhood death. *Still Standing Magazine* is a great platform to help guide you to other methods of support.

There are pages specific to certain topics and many resource pages. Sometimes the support is as simple as knowing you aren't alone in this journey.

*Reconceiving Loss* is an online support and resource center for anyone who has suffered the loss of a pregnancy or infant. There is an abundance of information on this website including material from their contributing psychologist, as well as media and book recommendations that may be of interest to you. The healing community created within this website encourages you to take care of your heart through many avenues of connection: essays, yoga, writing and photography. It also offers a sacred space to submit your story or to read the stories of others who have walked a similar experience.

**Local Resources:** Your hospital may be the best touchpoint to receive support after returning home without baby. They may have referrals that they can offer to local support groups. If not, there are nationwide programs, such as Compassionate Friends and the MISS Foundation, that have local chapters. See their website for more details and to explore if a group exists in your area. Other groups offer telephone support and can be available at any time.

**Counseling:** You may feel that counseling is the best option for you or for you and your family. There are many types of counseling. If you feel counseling isn't working, be sure to try more than one counselor before stopping. It may just be you haven't found the right professional to work with yet. Counseling can be individual, with a partner, as a family or as part of a support group led by a trained therapist. The intent is to support you in your emotional needs at a pace that is comfortable for you, and for whatever you may need to explore. It may just be that you need reassurance that what you are experiencing emotionally and physically as a result of grief, is normal. Counseling can also help parents or a family learn how to have empathy for those around you who are also learning to live with their broken hearts, just as you are learning to live with yours. Grief doesn't always bring out the best in people and it can be helpful to have someone guide you through these huge changes.

**Retreats:** Retreats that support healing can be found for bereaved mothers, fathers and/or families as a whole. Some are created with certain parameters, such as what diagnosis your baby had and some are solely to offer support now that your family has endured a tremendous loss. These organized groups facilitate the meeting of other bereaved individuals and gently allow you to make connections while being guided through taking care of yourself. Healing retreats can be a foundation of creating lifelong relationships of support far after the retreat has ended.

# SIX

## Re-entering the "Real" World

# Returning to the Life You Had: Returning to Work, Packing Baby's Things

LIFE NO LONGER CONSISTS OF THE FUTURE you planned, but now the people around you are expecting or waiting for you to return to a life that has not changed for them. Chances are, when you look in the mirror, you don't even recognize the face looking back at you—you are that different. You are no longer the person that you were when anxiously awaiting the arrival of your child, you never will be again and that is ok. Your life has irreparably changed and you get to decide what your new life will look like and who you want to be in this new "real" world.

Please do not feel pressured by anyone to do anything. When (or if) you return to work, when (or if) you pack up your baby's things, when (or if) you choose to resume the activities you had in your life before baby—all of that is up to you! You probably aren't sure what that's going to look like right now, THAT is also ok—do nothing until you are comfortable. You do not need to have all the answers right now, and you may never have all of the answers.

This life that you are now living is sometimes referred to as the "new normal". You can decide whether you want to adopt that term or not. The new normal insinuates that this is not the life that you planned but it is now your life, even though it FEELS anything but normal. While you didn't choose this path, you get to choose what your life is going to look like, including who will be along for your journey and how you show up in the world. I know you would have never chosen this situation, but this is where you are now. BE here, SIT here, figure out who you are and take your time doing so. There is no timeline to this process and there is no rush (other than monetary obligations, which, unfortunately, do determine our choices). Tend to your heart and be in this time that you never get back, the space when grief is so close and the memory of your child is so fresh. Savor these painful moments before the duties of life have set back in. And if you do have other children at home or a job that you must return to, be sure to carve out the space to be YOU, the mom who is grieving her broken heart. Take the time on the weekends or evenings to tend to you after all the other obligations are through for the day.

**Returning to Work:** Returning to work will throw you directly back to the world you left before your baby died, only your life is suddenly so very different. This is a huge choice and often, once it is made, it cannot be unmade. In many cases, one can take a catastrophic leave of absence, but once you say that you are ready to return to work, your employer will assume you are ready to go and your leave evaporates. It is important, as with all decisions during this sensitive time, that you make this choice thoughtfully and carefully.

The first thing to consider is that you just had a baby. Even though your baby is no longer here with you, your body has a lot of healing to do. In a typical birth, a woman's body needs 6-8 weeks of recovery time and she usually takes at least that much maternity leave—you are still entitled to that time. Take it. Even though you may feel as if the distraction of work will be beneficial, it is important to let your body heal, as well as your emotions.

If after that time, you feel ready to return to work, ask yourself the following questions:

- How will I feel facing my colleagues each day?
- Am I ready to interact with customers, clients, patients, and students?
- Do I sleep enough at night to fuel my body to work each day?
- Will the hours I have outside of my employment be enough to tend to my heart?
- Is my partner supportive of my return to work?
- Do I feel ready to work or do I feel pressured to work?
- Do I need to return to work?
- Do I want to return to work?
- Is it possible to return to work part-time?

You may find in your questioning that not only do you not want to return to work right now, but that you may never want to return to the line of work that you are in. That is a huge decision to make in this vulnerable time, but please listen to that voice inside you. Sometimes in the midst of great tragedy we are able to see things more clearly, and how we spend our daily lives is an important thing to reassess. You may just need a longer break from your line of work or you may now have the courage to explore something else that has always called to your heart. You now know that life is short; take advantage of every moment you have whether that means returning to a job you love, taking an extended leave to tend to your soul or finding the job that fuels your heart. Only you know what the right answer is and I hope that you are able (financially*) to do what's best for you.

*Check your insurance/disability policy to see if it covers catastrophic leave to help with finances during this time.

**Packing Up Baby's Things:** The baby's room (or space) that you created is a sacred place now. Each item that you chose or that was gifted to you was with the plan that you would be bringing home your living child. There is no rush or reason to pack up your baby's things. There is no right or wrong or timeline of when you are supposed to do this. These are big decisions and should not be rushed. Take time to think through how you will feel coming home to a complete baby room. Will it be a place of comfort and remembrance or will it create anxiety? As in everything related to the death of a baby, there are no rules except to do what you feel is right.

Some families choose to pack up the baby's room before they come home from the hospital because the thought of seeing a furnished but unused baby's room is too much to bear on an already broken heart. If you choose to pack it up, you may want to have photos of the room before breaking it down. This may or may not sound appealing but the photos may be something to share with future children, other family members or to help with your grieving process down the line. When you do pack the room up, you may want to do it alone or you may choose to have someone you trust do it for you. You may want to keep the items in storage for future children or you may want to donate the items. Both choices are completely normal and both are completely understandable.

Some families choose to keep the room intact for as long as they feel comfortable. Some leave the room until they are ready to have another child, the connection of their baby sharing items with a younger sibling is of comfort to them. Until then, a place that was filled with so much hope may now become a place of remembrance. You might like to sit in that room to feel close to your baby, or use it as a place to safely let your emotions flow. When people visit, you might want to share baby's room with them.

Whatever you decide, take your time. Follow your heart, listen to your gut and do what feels best. You can always close the door until you have decided what you would like to do. It is better to do nothing and wait, then to make a hasty decision that you may regret later.

# Sharing News in the Real World: "Grocery Store" Conversations, Alerting Others of Your Loss

You were pregnant the last time many people saw you at the places you frequent, whether at the grocery store, gym, library, bank or dentist. Now, unless these groups of people are also in your social circle, they probably have no idea of the traumatic loss that you have just experienced. You will find that you are encountering some uncomfortable conversations when you re-enter the real world. People don't mean to be insensitive, they often don't know how loaded the question is that they are asking. Questions that are typically asked:

- How is your baby?
- How are you doing?
- How many children do you have?

Everybody's comfort and level of sharing differs. Some people share all information about their child because they want to speak about their baby. Others may not share any information or even mention their child because the experience feels so sacred and personal. It does not mean anything about the love for your child if you decide to share everything or nothing at all.

Being prepared to answer these questions can help to ease the anxiety of being put on the spot. Knowing what you feel comfortable saying and what information you need others to know are things to consider. Sometimes, you will decide on a particular way to answer a question but when caught in the moment, find yourself frozen and without words. Having a prepared answer can really save you in these situations. You can act these out with your partner or trusted friend, write them out, re-play them in your head and perfect them with more practice and over time.

**"Grocery Store" Conversations:** Grocery store conversations is an umbrella term for situations that you might encounter when you are in the line at the grocery store, bank, gym or dentist—places that you have small talk while waiting, but with people that you might not necessarily see again. In these moments, you might alter your answers depending on the situation. Sometimes these moments pass so quickly, the question is asked, the words fall out and you walk away obsessing over how you answered, what you said, wondering if it was too much or not enough?

It is up to you how much you care to share with the person inquiring. You may choose to be completely forthcoming or subtler in your responses, and your choice of words may vary depending on the situation. You may choose to not share at all with this person and that is completely understandable. Your child is sacred, special and precious—some parents decide not to share because they don't feel the questioning party is privileged to learn about their baby. Whether you share or don't share, your baby is loved through and through.

When you are unprepared to speak about your baby, some simple "grocery store" responses to any question can be:

*"I know you aren't aware and I don't want you to feel badly, but we lost the baby and I am not ready to talk about it yet"*

*"Our baby passed away. We are still devastated & I am not comfortable talking about it yet."*

For those who choose to share, here are some grocery store responses to typical questions you may be asked:

(Seeing you after being pregnant)

*Q: Congratulations! How is the baby?*

*A: My daughter passed away at (<u>33 days old</u>).*

*(If accompanied by your other child)*

*Q: Is he/she your only child?*

*A: No, he has a sister.*

*Q: Do you have other children?*
*A: I do! I have a daughter, as well.*

Many times if you answer "yes," they'll continue to ask about your other child. If they push the questioning further, you get to choose how to proceed.

*Q: How old is your other child?*
*A: My daughter lived 33 days. Thanks for asking, I love speaking about her.*

(Later, in a subsequent pregnancy)
*Q: How many children do you have?*
*A: I have two.*
*Q: How old are they?*
*A: My daughter lived 33 days and my son is 3 1/2.*

*Q: Is this your first child?*
*A: No, second.*
*Q: How old is your first?*
*A: My daughter lived for 33 days.*
*Q: I'm so sorry.*
*A: Thank you —and don't feel sorry, I love speaking about her.*

The line "I love speaking about her" creates the opportunity for the person to inquire more if they desire. It gives them permission to know that you want to talk about your baby and sometimes it encourages the conversation to take a different turn. Your vulnerability in sharing your life experience allows the other person to share their experience of loss as well. This encounter gives the questioner the opportunity to share something they may not often speak about with another person. It is so magical when two people come together and can be authentic with one another.

Whether you want to be more specific, is completely up to you. These interactions usually last only a minute or two at the checkout counter, or in line at the bank and the moment is so fleeting. These simply put responses will either open the conversation further or shut it down quickly, if that's what you're hoping for.

I would encourage you to practice these statements with a trusted person. Saying them more than once (and not in "the moment") will help to ease the answers when you're truly in these situations. I'm not saying that you won't trip over your words in these conversations. Those nerves in your stomach will be there for a long time (if not always) and you can never be quite certain how the other person will react. Chances are, tears may well in your eyes and you may even walk away crying, but when you do choose to share your baby, you make your baby's imprint on another person's heart.

**Alerting Others of Your Loss:** For places that you frequent regularly, you may want to inform people there of your loss BEFORE you see them for the first time to ease any nerves you may be feeling. Below is a sample letter that you can reformat to apply to your own personal experience:

*Dear dentist,*

*When you last saw me, I was awaiting the birth of my precious baby girl, Ruthie Lou. I am writing to inform you that on September 10th, my beautiful child died. It was (un)expected and my family is grieving tremendously.*

*It is important for me to tell you before I return for my next appointment that although she is no longer with us, I love to speak her name and am very comfortable sharing about her brief life. Will you please share this information with your office staff?*

*Thank you so much for your kindness as we find our way back into the real world.*

*Sincerely,*

*Amie*

Perhaps you aren't comfortable speaking of your child upon your return. That is ok, too. Here is another option:

*Dear dentist,*

*When you last saw me, I was awaiting the birth of my precious baby girl, Ruthie Lou. I am writing to inform you that on September 10th, my beautiful child died. It was (un)expected and my family is grieving tremendously.*

*It is important for me to tell you, before I return for my next appointment, that we are still trying to navigate and come to terms with our loss. At this time, I am not comfortable sharing about her brief life. Will you please inform your office staff?*

*Thank you so much for your kindness as we find our way back into the real world.*

*Sincerely,*

*Amie*

It is also ok if you never go back to any of the places you frequented. Many people make that choice to protect their hearts.

## Relationship Changes

Support can be found in the unlikeliest places and even from friends and loved ones who have not directly experienced this type of loss. It may be the person you expected it to be, or it may be someone completely unexpected. If you have a trusted person who can sit in your grief with you, that is an enormous gift.

Many bereaved parents report that their families were not supportive or understanding of their grief. One thing that is easily overlooked, especially when considering the actions of your loved ones, is that their hearts are broken, too. Obviously, your child is your direct loss and their pain is of no comparison to yours, but sometimes the internal pain with which they are struggling prohibits them from being the best support to you. Trying to keep an open and honest line of communication is the best strategy. They may do or say things that feel inappropriate to you, but if they are doing anything at all (even when it hurts), it means that they are trying. They may not realize how their actions are hurting you. They may not make the best choice, or may not be what you asked for, but if they are continuing to show up, it means they are still in this with you.

Often we find that people want to help, but don't know how. This is through no fault of their own. Unless they have suffered their own deep loss (of some sort), many times they just don't know the right thing to do or say. It may feel like adding insult to injury when, not only are you grieving, you must also help friends or family know how to support you. The reality is that no two grievers are the same and those around you cannot know what you need unless you voice it to them. As hurtful as some of their well-intentioned comments can be, try to remember that they love you and are doing the best they can in the most devastating of circumstances.

Some people in your social circle (including family and close friends) may not show up in the way that you want them to or they may not show up at all. While this secondary loss can feel lonely, confusing and hurtful, it most likely has nothing to do with you, but more to do with their inability to handle this new reality. It is not always clear why someone can't show up for you when you need them. Your loss may bring up old hurts or fears. They may feel overwhelmed as to how to support you. They may not be able to sit with your grief. Many times they don't even know the actual reason themselves. Regardless, it hurts when those relationships you thought were unconditional, feel conditional. But, this isn't about you, it is about them. Repeat that to yourself and know that this condition may or may not be temporary. Extreme loss like yours changes everything, including other relationships.

There are also times when you may have voiced your needs and it feels too much to manage the relationship on top of tending to your own heart. It is ok to take a step back. This choice can be communicated or not, but it is acceptable to put yourself first. Your life just irreparably changed and you get to process that for as long as you need. It doesn't have to be a permanent decision regarding the relationship; perhaps you just need to take a break.

The best-case scenario is that you actually know what you need, you can communicate it and your loved ones can hear you and respond appropriately. Unfortunately, grief is usually not as simple as that. The emotions of grief are so overwhelming that most people would rather ignore, stuff or placate those feelings and move on. However, the healthiest thing to do is to move through the pain, to feel it and to heal, not push it aside.

Hopefully, you will find that you do have someone that can be of support to you. If not, please reach out to find help in other areas such as a support group, an online resource or a retreat with other families like yours.

## How to Protect Your Heart: Boundaries, Pregnancies, Baby Showers, Birthdays, Other Bereaved Parents

**Know Your Boundaries:** There are many things that can trigger your grief. Many parents have found that baby showers, other's pregnancies and life events such as birthdays, graduations and weddings can trigger grief regarding the future you will not have with your baby. It is important to know your boundaries and be able to allow yourself the grace of letting go of expectations that others may have placed on you or that you have placed on yourself. Sometimes, you may fall upon an event or situation you thought would be ok, only to find out that in fact you are definitely *not* ok! Listen to yourself and forgive yourself in those moments. If you need to politely excuse yourself from a situation, do so immediately. If you can't bring yourself to explain, just quietly slip out to clear your heart and mind. You do not owe anyone an explanation. Your true friends and family will love you regardless.

**Pregnancies:** Other women's pregnancies may or may not affect you, but be sure not to judge yourself either way or expect that it will always be the way you're feeling right now. You may find that being with a pregnant friend or family member is easy, but that a pregnant stranger is difficult. Or, the opposite could be true—you may feel that being by a pregnant stranger is easy, but that a pregnant friend or family member is difficult. You may find that all pregnant women affect you or none do. Be gentle with yourself in knowing that your only job right now is to allow yourself to feel through your emotions. These reactions may be temporary or long lasting and taking care of you is your priority.

**Baby Showers:** Baby showers are a symbol of hope, a symbol of the life growing inside a mothers' swollen belly and whether or not you had a baby shower for your child, other baby showers can be a trigger. Some women have found that they avoid any baby shower except those held for other bereaved mamas, close friends or family members. For other women, baby showers still hold the same beauty and hope that they once did and continue to be a wonderful thing to enjoy. The key is to trust your heart. When you receive the invitation in the mail, that initial feeling (whether positive or negative) can be very indicative of how you ultimately feel regarding the event. It is important to trust that feeling without judgement or the need to persuade yourself any other way.

Baby showers are a tricky time for all involved. Chances are inviting a woman whose baby has died was a decision that the person of honor did not choose lightly.

While receiving an invitation to a baby shower can bring up a lot of emotions about your own loss, it's important to see the best in others. Remember, your friends and family love you so much that they want to share their life with you. Those including you in their events are giving you the choice to do what feels safest to you. If it is someone you hold dear, it is a great opportunity to practice a tough conversation—sharing your fears about attending. It may also be a chance for you to attend a shower where the person of honor will hold a safe space for you.

It is ok to skip these events, just as it is ok to attend these events. If you choose to decline, the most polite way would be to RSVP that you won't be in attendance. However, you do not need to worry about being polite right now if a phone call, email or text feels too heavy a weight to bear. Should you choose to RSVP, no reason is necessary, it can be as simple as stating "I am unable to attend. Thank you for including me."

If you choose to attend, be clear with yourself (and the person of honor, if you desire) that if at any time you need to step away or leave, you may. Take care of you, first and foremost. Love your tender heart and listen to what YOU need. You may find that the day is sweet and you survive without incident, giving you courage to try again. You may also find that you weren't quite ready yet and that is ok, too.

**Birthdays:** Many families have found that birthday

parties for children born near the same time as your baby can be challenging. Each year that passes, a birthday represents the age and developmental stage of your child. This thought can prove to feel comforting for some, or heartbreaking to others. As with any thing that has been discussed in this handbook, trust yourself. Listen to your intuition and do what you feel is best for you. What you feel one year may be different from the next and you can reassess with every invitation.

Should you choose to attend a birthday, remind your brain to be in the present moment. If you find that your mind is wandering, comparing or leading you down an emotional path that you prefer not to go, breathe. Remind yourself of the reason(s) you chose to attend the party and regain your composure. It's also acceptable to go to the closest private spot and lose it, if you feel safe to do so. There is no Academy Award for being the best grieving actor. You may find that the release is just what you needed to do to proceed with the day.

**Other Bereaved Parents:** Having relationships with other bereaved parents may prove to be the best thing to help heal your heart. To find your tribe who can be supportive and find comfort with people who (although their journey and experience may be very different) can empathize with a greater understanding the depth of your grief can be very positive. You may also discover that although there are other parents with whom you share this loss, it may be the only thing you have in common and that may not be enough to sustain a relationship. It is ok to not become friends with every bereaved mom that you encounter. You will want to find others similar to you and perhaps where you are at on your particular journey. If you find that you feel triggered by other bereaved parents (whatever that might look like for you), it is ok to take a step back. This is not the time to worry about fostering relationships. You are the top priority. Should you find a person, or group of people that you connect with, stick with them! They will understand you in ways that others never will.

# Taking Care of You—Emotional Well-Being & Health: Food, Exercise, Ritual, Meditation, Creativity

Taking care of yourself is the best line of defense while you are grieving the loss of your child. You have lost the thing most precious to you and this loss stays with you for life. It will not always look the same, it will not always feel as overwhelming, but grief is such a heavy burden to bear. Grief is not linear, and there is no timeline for how long it lasts. Each person has her own unique experience. The feelings of loss, despair and sadness will ebb and flow, feel stronger or softer at unexpected times. You will think, grieve, heal and experience life more clearly if you can do things that will tend to your heart.

**Food:** Depending on the way you were raised or the coping mechanisms that you have relied on in your life, food during grief may be a difficult one for you to tackle. For some, unhealthy food and eating habits can be an emotional crutch. Grief can also grip so tightly on your heart that your reaction is to avoid food altogether. It is important to remember that grieving takes enormous energy and energy expelled is reliant upon calories consumed. It is important not only that you eat regularly, but that you eat nutritious food that will fuel your body. Food directly affects all parts of our bodies, including our emotions. When nutrient-dense food is consumed, your body is being prepared to best take care of itself.

Making a meal plan of what to eat is your best course of action to support healthy eating. Having healthy foods on hand in your cabinets and refrigerator will also make it easier for you to grab something from your kitchen rather than feeling the urge to eat convenience foods.

One option is to dedicate a small amount of time to food prepping each week. In a short time on the weekend, you can prepare a large batch of oatmeal for daily breakfasts, soup or pre-prepped salads for lunch and staples such as potatoes, rice, beans or quinoa to be quick side dishes to pair with a protein for dinner. Having these items available to you will help make mealtime less overwhelming and an easier way to consume healthy, nourishing food. If you don't feel capable of completing the shopping, prep work and cooking for you and/or your family, then a meal delivery service may be a better choice for you. You will still have to cook the meal, but the planning, organizing and shopping are done for you.

**Exercise:** Exercise is beneficial to your emotional well-being. Whether you belong to a gym or you take a slow stroll outside, exercise helps you emotionally, and can also help with the physical effects of grief such as headaches, fatigue and sleep disturbances. When you exercise, you increase circulation and blood flow, helping to build your immune system. This is even better when you are outside, breathing fresh air!

Those who exercise have an image of control in a time when life feels out of control, helping to give you strength during this really overwhelming time. Exercising stimulates the production of new neurons including those that help to induce a natural state of calm. It also allows you time to think and process in an active environment. If you are working out solo, you have time while swimming, walking or cycling to think through things in a more focused manner than if you were occupied by other duties. Exercise allows an emotional release that you may not feel safe having otherwise. Many people are surprised to find they are able to cry more freely while exercising.

**Ritual:** Rituals are acts that are created and performed by an individual in any type of setting. Some people create rituals to deal with anxiety producing activities such as public speaking, performing or any daily activity that causes angst. Grievers often create ritualistic behaviors to maintain a sense of relationship with the loved one who has died, to find a sense of peace with their loss or to gain some sort of control when life feels completely out of control.

Rituals are a personal act, sometimes created without even being aware of what is happening. Mostly, rituals are perfectly healthy and a comfortable, safe way to include your baby in your daily life. Some rituals may include visiting your baby's graveside, or lighting a candle at home. These rituals can be daily, weekly or on special occasions such as baby's birthday or anniversary dates. Rituals often give a sense of parenting your baby when you can no longer physically be with them.

There are other rituals that are beneficial to your emotional health and that are widely used as a healing part of your grief journey. These can include creating a special place to sit and meditate, writing in a journal or a daily tea practice that encourages reflection. All of these acts provide a safe place to connect with your heart. Sometimes, that few minutes of reflection is all that time permits during the return to your life and it is important to give yourself that space.

*Teamotions* is a tea company that began after the unexpected death of the founder's twin daughters as a way to provide comfort and support physical and emotional well-being. The motivation for this company is to normalize all the systems of your body by using adaptogen herbs backed by science and tradition, so your body can heal itself. When you sit with a warm cup of tea, it allows you the space to just "be" and to listen to what your heart needs.

The only time that you need to be concerned about a ritualistic behavior is if it has overshadowed your daily life, prohibiting you from participating in activities or if you are using your rituals to avoid grief and the grieving process. If you find that you are unable to perform life duties until your rituals are completed, this would be a good thing to discuss with a counselor or therapist. It doesn't mean that there is anything wrong with what you are doing or that you have to stop the ritual, you just want to be healthy in your grief process. Sometimes being healthy includes using the help of a professional to find balance.

**Meditation:** Meditation is used to calm the mind and relax your body, and can be so beneficial in your grief journey. To learn to meditate, you can read a book, take a class or listen to a guided meditation. Like exercise, meditation reduces pain, boosts the immune system and increases concentration and focus. The brain can get so clouded in grief that it feels out of control, as if someone else is running your emotions. Meditation encourages all those thoughts and feelings to be set aside, allowing one to focus on a calm place with love and light.

Meditation can be helpful no matter where you are in your grieving journey, new or years down the road.

Simple techniques using observation, breathing into the current moment and learning to stay present can help ground you. This doesn't mean that if you attain a certain level of Zen that your grief will subside and all will be healed. However, this practice can give you a reprieve from the continuous voices in your head that are replaying your loss over and over again. Meditation can help center you on days and during times when you need to be reminded to breathe. This is merely another tool from the toolbox to take care of yourself.

**Creativity:** Creativity allows for an emotional outlet when you cannot find the words or they just don't suffice. Being creative means many things and can take on various art forms. Even those who believe that they don't possess one creative bone in their body are surprised to know that expressing yourself with an artistic outlet can feel incredibly healing. Don't focus on the outcome or final product of your art, be present in the moment for whatever your heart is guiding your brain to create.

Creating an artful expression can also be a way to redefine who you are after the death of your child. When a person experiences a loss of this magnitude, it rocks them to the core of their being, leaving them to question how to make sense of the world and their new place in it. Art as an expression of grief can help guide you to discover who you are and what you envision your life to look like since your world has changed so suddenly.

There are many ways to use art as a medium (as listed

below). If you're reading this list but you don't know where to start, take a class, watch videos on YouTube or ask a friend who can teach you. The idea is to take your energy and focus it on something that can be tangible.

Here are some creative ideas to investigate:

- Create a collage
- Paint—watercolors, acrylic, pottery
- Mosaic
- Draw
- Create and /or color a mandala
- Sculpt
- Craft
- Scrapbook
- Knit
- Sew
- Quilt
- Photography
- Sing
- Compose music
- Dance
- Yoga
- Garden
- Play an instrument
- Write poetry
- Journal your thoughts
- Collect quotes

- Write a letter to your baby
- Narrate your baby's life story

# SEVEN

The Future

# Firsts: Birthdays, Anniversaries, Holidays

THE FIRSTS WITHOUT YOUR BABY can be unpredictable. The unknowns of the day, not knowing how you might feel combined with the imagining what might have been, can be emotionally taxing. Every year will look different, but there are some ways to include your baby in these special occasions. Your goal is to find what feels right to you. Some years that may include doing nothing. You may want to share the special day with the world. You may feel safer closing yourself in from the outside for the day. How to celebrate, honor or memorialize your baby is fluid and what you choose to do one year may not feel right the next. Follow your heart and intuition to know what is best for you and your family.

During the holidays we are usually surrounded with joyful people. This may be a time that you are not feeling filled with joy. Protect your heart by choosing to be surrounded by those who are sensitive to your grief. Consider having a conversation with the host prior to the event about how you might feel that day and that you may not stay for the entire gathering. Those who love you, although they may not understand, will support and accept you. As for those who don't empathize, you may want to reconsider spending such a sensitive day with them.

Be prepared on these days to experience unexpected emotions. Whether these emotions are surprisingly peaceful or unpredictably anger filled, they are the body's way of processing something foreign. Acknowledge that you are processing your grief and although it can be surprising and uncomfortable, it is healthy.

Here are ways in which some families honor their child during special days:

**Birthdays & Anniversaries:**

- Light a candle
- Buy balloons to keep or release
- Send notes in a helium balloon
- Release sky lanterns
- Release butterflies or ladybugs
- Eat delicious dessert, cake or cupcakes
- Sing Happy Birthday
- Sift through pictures
- Create a piece of art or a craft
- Make a digital slideshow or photo collage
- Write your child a letter
- Start a blog
- Create a foundation or non-profit
- Get a tattoo
- Invite family/friends to celebrate
- Spend the day with your partner and other children
- Be in nature
- Participate in a Kindness Project

- Donate in honor of your child
- Give to a family in need with a child of similar age to yours

**Father's & Mother's Day**:

- Light a candle
- Talk to your baby
- Write to your baby
- Write publicly about your baby for others to read
- Write privately in a journal
- Plant a memorial plant, flower, garden
- Be in nature
- Surround yourself with support
- Spend time alone
- Eat your most favorite foods

**Thanksgiving:**

- Create a gratitude list
- Ask family to create a page for a "thankful" scrapbook
- Light a candle during the meal
- Include a photo or symbolic item in the gathering area
- Speak your child's name when sharing what you are grateful for

**Christmas:**
- Light a candle at home
- Light a candle at church
- Hang a stocking
- Fill stocking with letters from family
- Buy a donation gift for a child of similar age
- "Adopt" a family for Christmas
- Include your child's name, photo or symbol on your holiday card

**Valentine's Day:**
- Write your baby a love letter
- Include your baby's name in your card/gift to your partner
- Buy flowers in honor of your baby

**Easter:**
- Create an Easter basket for your baby
- Write baby's name on colored eggs
- Light a candle at home
- Light a candle at mass/church

Also, know that it is ok to do nothing on holidays and anniversaries. You can choose to celebrate holidays without mention of your child or not acknowledge those days at all. You love and miss your baby every day and you carry her with you always. There may not be a need to create a separate acknowledgement of her on these days—she is always a part of your every day.

# Memorializing Your Child

Memorializing your child is one way that many parents keep their child's memory alive; it helps to process grief and also leaves a mark on the world since they not here to do so themselves. There are various reasons people choose to memorialize their child. Many times it is to create meaning to this tragedy and to make the world a better place in their child's memory. It may be for personal reasons, it may be to help brothers and sisters to understand that their sibling's life was special, it may be for the world to know that their baby is loved and forever missed. It doesn't matter the reasons in which you choose to memorialize your child, what matters is that what you choose feels good to you and is never forced upon you.

Sometimes, well-intentioned family or friends will do or create things in honor of your child for you. Although a beautiful gesture, if for some reason the item makes you feel uncomfortable or is upsetting, it is perfectly ok to place it in storage. It does not need to be displayed and the person who gifted the item doesn't need to know. The intention of these gifts is to show support and love, the gifter would want you to do what best takes care of your heart.

Truly, our children are memorialized in our everyday living of life, but here are some ideas that families do to include their child and (externally) memorialize them:

- Send birth announcements
- Send cards to friends/family on baby's birthday
- Keep a journal
- Design jewelry to wear including your child's name, picture or a symbol
- Sponsor a park bench
- Engrave a brick in your local area
- Plant a tree in a public area
- Donate books to hospitals or libraries in honor of your child
- If buried—clean, maintain and decorate your child's grave
- Light a candle in the evenings when at home
- Include your child's photo (or memorial art) on the wall
- Create collages to process emotions at different times of the year(s)
- Run a memorial tribute in your local newspaper during special days
- Hang bird feeders to invite favorite birds to your yard
- Plant a special garden in your backyard
- Hang wind chimes, feel your baby close to your heart
- Collect special items, symbolic of your

child—share that symbol with others so they can do the same

- Order a weighted item (bear, heart, blanket) to hold or sleep with
- Order memorial photos of your baby's name in nature (Seashore of Remembrance)
- Photograph symbolic items that you come across in nature
- Write baby's name in the sand
- Quilt or create a blanket or bear with baby's special clothes
- Name a star after your baby
- Have a special place (shelf or alter) to display keepsakes
- Create a memory box with baby's special items
- Participate in local memorial events
- Fundraise for a charity that supports child loss
- Make a charitable contribution in honor of your child
- Take a creative course that interests you

# Growing Your Family: Do We vs. Can We? Genetic Testing, No More Children, Subsequent Pregnancy

**Do We/Can We Have Another Baby?** The question of "do we" vs. "can we" when considering another pregnancy can feel like a cruel joke after your baby has died. Wanting or not wanting to consider another child, is perfectly normal. Your body, hormones and heart are trying to process this unthinkable loss and there is no right or wrong here. You may not even know (yet) if having another child is possible, so there is much to consider here.

When considering whether or not to have more children, you and your partner may have very different perspectives, unique fears and legitimate concerns. Adding to your family is a hugely personal question, one that is never taken lightly and is a decision that fills entire books! You and your partner may not agree on how to proceed with your family after experiencing such a horrendous loss. One of you may want more children immediately while the other may feel too scared to ever even consider having another child.

Take time to talk to one another about this decision, openly and without judgement. It is important to know where your partner is coming from and to be aware of what he/she is experiencing. This may be difficult to do with a verbal conversation. To be sure all your thoughts are expressed adequately, some couples find it easier to communicate through writing or it also may be necessary to have a neutral third person with you while you talk. A trusted confidante or a licensed therapist can help guide the conversation in a safe manner. These conversations are emotional and personal but so important. You both love your baby, but your experience of loss is being felt very differently. Be patient with each other and be respectful of one another's experience.

**Genetic Testing:** When your child died, you may or may not have been given insight as to the cause of her death. Lack of information can be extremely concerning when considering growing your family and can cause tremendous fear regarding a subsequent pregnancy. Even for those who do know the cause of their child's death, there may still be apprehension. In either case, you may want to consider having genetic testing for you and your partner to help guide your decision making, or to be most informed when you decide which direction to proceed.

Genetic testing is a medical test that looks at your chromosomes, genes and/or proteins to determine if you or your partner are carriers of any genetic conditions, particularly if one contributed to your child's diagnosis. This procedure can be done at a lab by administering a simple blood draw with results returned in approximately 2 weeks. The results will give you information about the statistical probability of contributing any genetic conditions to future children. The genetic information may or may not change your decision about having another child, but it can prepare you for possible scenarios in future pregnancies. On the contrary, genetic results may reassure you to know that statistically speaking your chances of having a healthy baby are the same as the general public. If you complete genetic testing and find that you are in fact a carrier, it doesn't necessarily mean that your child will be diagnosed with a particular disorder. It will, however, present you the statistics to best inform you when making future decisions with your partner.

In addition to your desire to have more children, you may not know if you can physically have more children. If you find that you are unable to carry another pregnancy, this can create an additional sense of loss. There are options for a woman who finds that she cannot carry the pregnancy herself (surrogacy, adoption). These are large decisions that will take time especially when they not have previously been considered.

Some families decide, that while they may be physically capable to carry another pregnancy with risks equal to the general public, they will not to grow their family. There are numerous reasons that families choose to live childfree and that is a decision that needs no defending. For other families, there is no question about wanting to have a (living) child, and that decision deserves equal empathy and understanding.

Options and choices regarding growing your family are personal and huge life altering decisions with many considerations. There are many unforeseen changes that a person encounters after the death of their baby, growing your family is only one of many changes. It can take time to come to a place of peace about this and that is ok. Finding that you cannot continue to grow your family in the way that you desire or once imagined is devastating. There is, however, a community of others who can help offer advice, experience, resources and support should you be looking for input. Having the support of others can be a powerful tool of comfort as you navigate this unknown time.

**No More Children:** Whether by choice or because you are unable, you may find that you will not have any more children after your baby has died. You may have had children prior to your loss, but for some, this baby may have been the first and only child. These are emotionally heavy and unique experiences and it is important to work through your grief in this secondary loss.

Those who love you may want to hold hope that you will have another child. To have to continuously explain, hear or have these conversations can be emotionally exhausting. Your loved ones only want what they feel is best for you and, unfortunately, you may not agree with them. Being able to have a gentle conversation with them may help you to explain your situation, but it is not necessary. Some will understand and hear you the first time but others may never hear your words and that can feel quite frustrating. Your situation or decision does not need to be understood or validated by others. It is only important that you and your partner agree and can support each other. Searching out a support group or community of other parents without living children may help you to find peace as you navigate this new life. It can be reassuring and helpful to find support from those who understand your situation.

**Subsequent Pregnancy:** Families who are physically able and decide to pursue a subsequent pregnancy may discover that even though you desire continuing to grow your family, this pregnancy may be more challenging than you experienced in pregnancies before your loss.

Your doctor may want to more closely monitor you this pregnancy, depending on the cause of death for your baby. For some, this additional monitoring is welcomed and appreciated and alleviates stress. For others, the additional hospital visits can be anxiety provoking. You will know what you feel most comfortable with and should do your research to learn what is most medically necessary in this pregnancy.

What might have been simple decisions in your previous pregnancy may carry more weight in a subsequent pregnancy. There are many things to consider when you are pregnant after loss. You may reconsider how you proceed this time, such as:

- Find out gender?
- Share gender news with family?
- Do you do prenatal testing?
- Have an amniocentesis?
- Have a baby shower?
- Prepare a nursery?
- Buy baby items?
- Deliver at home, in a hospital or a birthing center?

You may also find that during this pregnancy, others (who do and do not know your history) will ask the various innocent questions about your pregnancy, which can put you on the spot. This is a good opportunity to have prepared "grocery store" answers, as previously discussed.

- Is this your first?
- How many children do you have?
- How old are your other children?
- Will you do genetic testing?
- Is your (previous) child's condition hereditary?

No two pregnancies are the same, but bereaved moms can have a heightened sense of anxiety in pregnancies after a loss. Your emotional responses to this pregnancy are normal considering all that you have endured and it is important that you find support during this critical time. There are numerous resources available to you, both online and in the real world in the form of books, support groups and therapists.

# EIGHT

## Grief

THERE REALLY AREN'T WORDS ADEQUATE to express the grief and loss that you feel in your heart when your child has died. There is no way to do justice to the emptiness and agony that your soul is now experiencing. Your life as you knew it, as you had envisioned it, will never be the same. That knowledge is a huge burden to bear and to process logically and emotionally. The words written in the following section are not meant to demean or belittle the overwhelming emotions you are feeling, yet they are waiting here for when you are ready to read them, or in the times that you need the hope to know that you can survive this loss even if you are not quite there yet. Grief is a process, one that ebbs and flows like the tide of the ocean. As devastating and unbelievable as this sounds, you will experience love, joy and life again. Until then, feel every raw, painful and devastating emotion; it is ultimately how you will survive this. Feeling the feelings is the only way through and as much as it hurts, it will be best for your emotional well-being in the end.

# Experiencing Grief

Grief is the normal and natural response to loss, it does not discriminate, it knows no boundaries and nobody is immune. It is unpredictable, not limited in length of time and is unique to each individual. You have experienced the most heartbreaking loss any parent could ever imagine and this sorrow is now your reality. It will not go away, it will always be part of your life story and there will always be a missing piece of your heart in the shape of your child's love. Still there is hope. Hope may feel unbelievable to you, it may feel unattainable to you, but it is true if you allow it to be. Your life will not always feel this way.

Grief will last longer than others expect. Many times the depth of your grief will not become apparent until all the activity of those around you has quieted down, when the phone stops ringing and the visitors stop coming. Your loved ones and the people who care about you will want your pain to end because they love you and it is hard for them to feel so helpless. Some will be able to sit with you in your grief, some will have the patience to withstand the length of time that it takes to process this grief (which is much longer than one would think), but some might not walk by your side as you would hope or expect of them. This is normal and if this situation is true for you, then this is the time that you need to reach out for help beyond your social/family circle.

Grief is uncomfortable. You will act and react in ways that feel foreign and unexpected to the person you once were, the person you once knew. It can be scary, overwhelming and feel as if it will never end. For many, it is surprising how long life feels clouded with grief. Although grief is an emotional response, it includes and interrupts all parts of our physical body as well: sleeping, eating, normal life duties, the ability to concentrate, are all affected by grief. There is hope that these feelings and this lack of control over your emotions and body will subside over time. Some may argue that the grief doesn't go away, some will say that your grief will change with time, some say that you just learn to carry the grief with you. Your interpretation of grief is your own. You will find your own path on this journey. Please reach out for support and a soft place to land when you are ready.

You will learn that time is not the healer of your heart, you are. There are many programs that can help support you, some from parents whose children have died, others that focus on grief in general. There is support online, in person, in groups and through one-on-one services. You may feel more comfortable in one type than another, you may also find that you need the services of more than one kind and that is ok, too. You are responsible for your healing on this journey and you alone are the only one who can find peace in your heart. The more you open yourself up to the idea that you can find healing, the more likely that you will find it. It does not come easily, but it is possible and it is worth it. You are worth it.

## Grief and Your Partner

Your grief experience will be unique to you. Your partner's experience will look very different from yours because you both process grief differently. This can be a really challenging time in a relationship as you both grieve the loss of your baby. Chances are, your grief will look so different it will be unrecognizable to one another. It is hard to support each other when you are both hurting and having a hard time taking care of your own needs, let alone your partner's needs, too. Be gentle with each other. Give one another time to process without judgement. Communicate your emotions and give each other space when you need time to process. Just because it doesn't appear that your partner is suffering, doesn't mean that they are not in the same or similar pain to you. Remember that we all handle our emotions differently. Counseling, therapy or groups can save a relationship that is experiencing this traumatic loss. Be patient. This transition of your life can take longer to heal than you would expect, so give your relationship the time it needs to find its grounding again.

Every person manages grief differently. In a relationship, it is hard to be understanding and patient when grieving. There is no right or wrong way to grieve (as long as it is healthy), but it may feel deceiving if your partner is appearing to handle their loss differently than you. These differences do not mean that they are not hurting or in as much pain; they are finding their way through their grief just as you are and this can look very unfamiliar. Some people choose to keep busy, some prefer the quiet solitude. Some are criers, others never openly shed a tear. Some return to work, others never have the desire. Some are talkers and others will never utter their baby's name. Some make grand gestures to keep their baby's memory alive, others want to move on as if nothing happened. There is no way to know how you or your partner will react to this loss until you are actually in it. There is no way to prepare or protect your relationship except to have patience, love, respect and empathy for the other as they work through their pain.

The most important skill you can create in your relationship is communication. You may be able to accomplish this on your own, but most cannot. A professional neutral third party can help guide you and hold those important conversations in a safe space to hold the heavy weight that you both are carrying. It is sacred work, to find your way back to each other when grief has pulled you apart. You two are the only parents to your baby, you alone are the ones who were planning your child's life as a family and who love your baby more than life itself. It is so important to hold onto the love you had for each other, through the love of your child, and not allow the depths of your grief tear you apart. Here are some ways to stay connected or to re-connect in the most devastating season of your relationship:

- Be patient and gentle with your partner.

- Listen to each other.

- Make sure you're both staying nourished and hydrated. When you grab a snack, offer your partner a snack—they're probably hungry, too.

- Cook meals together for distracted quality time.

- Cook for your partner if they are not able to take care of their needs that day.

- Suggest a timeline of allowing sadness each day; how long you'll stay in bed or a long bath, etc.

- Give each other space to grieve but help your partner back when it's time for a break from the depths of sadness.

- Go to counseling together and listen to what your partner is experiencing.

- Go to counseling alone and allow your partner the privacy of not sharing what he/she shares with the counselor.

- If your partner writes, do not read your partner's journal unless asked.

- Ask to read your partners journal, having feelings in print might make it easier to communicate.

- Include your partner in your healing practices, but respect if he/she chooses not to participate.

- Write love notes to one another about your baby or about nothing at all.

- Spend time outside in nature together hiking, walking, cycling.

- Take time away from your home, whether it's a vacation or just a night or afternoon out— fresh air can be so healing.

- Find a creative outlet that you can enjoy together, whatever your common interests were before baby.

- Identify ways that you both prefer to honor your baby in your home, for the holidays, on special or difficult days and every day.

- Be patient if your partner is not ready or comfortable having sex.

- Be as intimate as you're comfortable experiencing; the time together will bring you closer.

- Hug. Even when you don't feel like it, hug one another, as it softens the jagged feelings of isolation.

## Your Grief Journey

Your grief may surprise you. You may not recognize yourself in the mirror. Your emotional responses may be unlike anything that you have ever experienced before. Ask for help. Look in any place that feels comfortable: a friend, a family member, a doctor, a therapist or a counselor. This is not the time to be brave or strong, this is the time to survive. Grief does not go away on its own and in order to move through it, you have to feel these dark feelings. You may have thoughts of suicide or wishing you would die—and this is really scary. Reach out. Tell someone. There is nothing wrong with you. The depths of these feelings will not last forever. Allow others to tend to you, to take care of you, to love you through this heartbreak and make sure to take gentle care of yourself, as well.

- Write in a journal.
- Spend time in nature.
- Be as active as possible, if even just a walk each day.
- Use art as a creative outlet.
- Give yourself limits of sadness each day, and then re-join the world for a portion of the day.
- Honor your baby in the ways that feel most comfortable to you.
- Speak your baby's name and share her story with supportive friends.
- Find a support group, either on-line or in person.
- Connect with other bereaved parents for understanding.
- Search and speak regularly with a counselor.

You will always love and miss your baby, but your grief will not always be this heavy. Take care of you, even if it is one small thing a day. You will experience love, peace and joy in your life again. This will take time, but it is possible. You deserve joy, love and life. You are worth it.

# RESOURCES

# Appendix

### Immediate Support

*A Gift of Time*, Amy Kuebelbeck and Deborah L. Davis, PhD

*Loving and Letting Go: For Parents Who Decided to Turn Away from Aggressive Medical Intervention for Their Critically Ill Newborns*, Deborah L. Davis, PhD

*Stillbirth, Yet Still Born*, Deborah L. Davis, PhD

*Unexpected Goodbye: When Your Baby Dies*, Angela Rodman


### Grief

*A Broken Heart Still Beats: After Your Child Dies*, Anne McCracken

*Dear Parents-Letters to Bereaved Parents, Centering Corporation For Bereaved Grandparents*, Margaret H. Gerner

*Grief…Reminders for Healing*, Gale Massey

*Grieving Parents, Surviving Loss as a Couple*, Nathalie Himmelrich

*The Grief Recovery Handbook*, John W. James & Russell Friedman

*Three Minus One: Stories of Parents' Love & Loss*, Sean Hanish & Brooke Warner

*Understanding Your Grief: Ten Essential Touchstones for Finding Hope and Healing Your Heart*, Alan D. Wolfelt

## Journals

*Family Lasts Forever: A Very Special Baby Book*, Noelle K. Andrew & Sheila B. Frascht

*Love Lasts Forever: A Journal of Memories*, Noelle K. Andrew & Sheila B. Frascht

*On Coming Alive: Journaling Through Grief*, Lexi Behrndt

## Memoirs

*A Piece of My Heart*, Molly Fumia

*An Exact Replica of a Figment of My Imagination*, Elizabeth McCracken

*Brona: A Memoir*, Mara Hill

*Expecting Adam*, Martha Beck

*Holding Silvan*, Monica Wesolowska

*I Will Carry You*, Angie Smith

*Laughing in a Waterfall*, Marianne Dietzel

*Silvie's Life*, Dr. Marianne Rogoff

*The Lessons of Love*, Melody Beattie

*What I Gave to the Fire*, Kim Flowers Evans

## Specific to Moms

*Sunshine After the Storm, A Survival Guide for the Grieving Mother*, Alexa Bigwarfe

*You Are Not Alone: Love Letters From Loss Mom to Loss Mom*, Emily Long

*You Are the Mother of All Mothers*, Angela Miller

*Invisible Mothers: When Love Doesn't Die*, Emily Long

## Specific to Dads

*A Guide for Fathers: When a Baby Dies*, Tim Nelson

*From Father to Father: Letters From Loss Dad to Loss Dad*, Emily Long

*Grieving Dads: To the Brink and Back*, Kelly Farley and David DiCola

*The Griefcase: A Man's Guide To Healing and Moving Forward In Grief*, R. Glenn Kelly

## Children's Books

*Healing Your Grieving Heart for Kids: 100 Practical Ideas*, Alan D. Wolfelt

*I Miss You: A First Look at Death*, Pat Thomas

*Lifetimes: The Beautiful Way to Explain Death to Children*, Bryan Mellonie and Robert Ingpen

*Someone Came Before You*, Pat Schwiebert

*Special Delivery*, Melanie Tioleco-Cheng

*The Invisible String*, Patrice Karst and Geoff Stevenson

*Tear Soup: A Recipe for Healing After Loss*, Pat Schwiebert and Chuck DeKlyen

*The Next Place*, Warren Hanson

## Pregnancy After Loss

*Celebrating Pregnancy Again*, Franchesca Cox

*Pregnancy After a Loss*, Carol Cirulli Lanham

## Philosophy, Psychology, Spiritual, Inspirational

*A Deep Breath of Life: Daily Inspiration for Heart Centered Living*, Alan Cohen

*A Grief Observed*, C.S. Lewis

*Brave Enough*, Cheryl Strayed

*Broken Open: How Difficult Times Can Help Us Grow*, Elizabeth Lesser

*Healing After Loss: Daily Meditations For Working Through Grief*, Martha Whitmore Hickman

*Healing Through the Dark Emotions: The Wisdom of Grief, Fear and Despair*, Miriam Greenspan

*Heaven is for Real*, Todd Burpo and Lynn Vincent

*Life Prayers from Around the World*, Elizabeth Roberts & Elias Amidon

*Something Like Magic: On Remembering How to be Alive*, Brian Andreas

*The Power of a Broken-Open Heart: Life-Affirming Wisdom from the Dying*, Julie Interrante, MA

*The Untethered Soul: The Journey Beyond Yourself*, Michael A. Singer

*To Bless the Space Between Us*, John O'Donohue

*When Bad Things Happen to Good People*, Harold S. Kushner

*Who Dies? An Investigation of Conscious Living and Conscious Dying*, Stephen and Ondrea Levine

# Bibliography

**Support Sites**

CaringBridge www.caringbridge.org

CarePages www.carepages.com

MyLifeLine www.mylifeline.org

YouCaring www.youcaring.com

GiveForward www.giveforward.com

GoFundMe www.gofundme.com

Give InKind www.giveinkind.com


**Perinatal Hospice**

Perinatal Hospice & Palliative Care

www.perinatalhospice.org/list-of-programs.html

Focus on the Family

www.focusonthefamily.com/lifechallenges/relationship
-challenges/when-your-baby-wont-survive/carrying-
your-baby-to-term

End of Life Content in Treatment Guidelines for Life-
Limiting Diseases

www.ncbi.nlm.nih.gov/pubmed/15684843

Information About Serious Illness

www.baylorhealth.com/SiteCollectionDocuments/Doc
uments_BHCS/BHCS_Patient%20Info_DocumentsForm
s/SeriousIllness_rev8.pdf

## Pediatric Palliative Care Facility

George Mark Children's House www.georgemark.org

Ryan House www.ryanhouse.org

## Delivering Hard News

Talking to Children About Death

www.hospicenet.org/html/talking.html

Death: How to Explain it to Children

www.nspt4kids.com/therapy/death-how-to-explain-it-to-children

Explaining to Young Children that Someone Has Died

www.childbereavementuk.org/files/5614/0117/9770/Explaining_to_young_children_that_someone_has_died.pdf

## After Death Arrangements

Pediatric Palliative Care

www.getpalliativecare.org/whatis/pediatric

Association of Organ Procurement www.aopo.org

Purposeful Gift www.purposefulgift.com

Institute for the Advancement of Medicine Neonatal Donation Program www.iiam.org/

Cuddle Cot www.flexmort.com/cuddle-cots

## Burial Gowns

NICI Helping Hands

www.nicuhelpinghands.org/programs/angel-gown-program

## Mortuary/Funeral Arrangements

Is there a difference between funeral home and a
mortuary?
www.sciencecare.com/blog-is-there-a-difference-
between-funeral-home-and-a-mortuary
What is the Difference between a Mortuary and a
Funeral Home? www.imortuary.com/blog/what-is-the-
difference-between-a-mortuary-and-a-funeral-home

## Autopsy

UF Health FAQ's: Autopsy
www.pathlabs.ufl.edu/services/autopsy/faq-autopsy
Regional Pathology and Autopsy Services
www.regional-pathology.com/faq

## Honoring Your Baby's Life

Funerals vs. Celebration of Life
www.johnsonsfuneralhome.com/Funerals_vs._Celebrati
ons_of_Life_1263241.html
Planning a Funeral or Memorial Service
www.sevenponds.com/after-death/planning-a-funeral-
or-memorial-service
Home Funerals Grow as American's Skip the Mortician
for After Death Care
www.huffingtonpost.com/2013/01/25/home-funerals-
death-mortician_n_2534934.html

National Home Funeral Alliance

www.homefuneralalliance.org

Funeral Consumers Alliance www.funerals.org

**Postnatal Care**

Mayo Clinic: C-Section Recovery

www.mayoclinic.org/healthy-lifestyle/labor-and-delivery/in-depth/c-section-recovery/art-20047310

Mayo Clinic: Postpartum Care

www.mayoclinic.org/healthy-lifestyle/labor-and-delivery/in-depth/postpartum-care/art-20047233

BabyCenter www.babycenter.com/0_recovering-from-a-c-section_221.bc

Parents Magazine

www.parents.com/pregnancy/giving-birth/cesarean/c-section-recovery-timeline-tips

The Bump: Vaginal Recovery

www.thebump.com/a/the-truth-about-postpartum-recovery-from-vaginal-delivery

The Bump: C-Section Recovery

www.thebump.com/a/care-recovery-after-c-section

**Online Resources & Emotional Support**

The Ruthie Lou Foundation

www.ruthieloufoundation.org

Still Standing Magazine www.stillstandingmag.com

Unspoken Grief www.unspokengrief.com

Reconceiving Loss www.reconceivingloss.com

Compassionate Friends www.compassionatefriends.org

The MISS Foundation www.missfoundation.org

HAND, Helping After Neonatal Death

www.handonline.org

Faces of Loss, Faces of Hope www.facesofloss.com

Shared Grief Project www.sharedgrief.org

Star Legacy Foundation www.starlegacyfoundation.org

The Grief Recovery Method

www.griefrecoverymethod.com

**Retreats**

Return to Zero Center for Healing

www.returntozerohealingcenter.com

Heal by Choice Cruise Retreats

www.healbychoicecruiseretreat.com

Faith's Lodge www.faithslodge.org

Respite Retreat www.nancyguthrie.com/respite-retreat

Landon's Legacy Retreat

www.landonslegacyretreat.com

Selah: MISS Foundation Retreat

www.missfoundation.org

**Meal Delivery Services**

Blue Apron www.blueapron.com

Green Chef www.greenchef.com

Hello Fresh www.hellofresh.com

Home Chef www.homechef.com

Peach Dish www.peachdish.com

Terra's Kitchen www.terraskitchen.com

**Taking Care of You**

How Exercise Can Help the Grieving Process

www.fitness.mercola.com/sites/fitness/archive/2014/06/2

7/exercise-grief.aspx

Sweating Out the Sadness

www.dailyburn.com/life/lifestyle/exercise-coping-with-

grief-sadness/

A Meditation on Grief

www.jackkornfield.com/meditation-grief/

How Meditation Helps You Cope with Grief

www.brainwave-research-institute.com/how-

meditation-helps-you-cope-with-grief.html

Meditation: Helpful to Those Who Grieve

www.griefhealingblog.com/2013/12/meditation-

helpful-to-those-who-grieve.html

You Aren't Here Now: How Grief and Mindfulness

Don't Mix www.huffingtonpost.com/megan-

devine/grief-and-mindfulness_b_4757042.html

Grief and Nutrition: Tips From A Wellness Guru

www.whatsyourgrief.com/grief-and-nutrition

Eight Healthy Coping Tips To Manage Grief
www.mysahana.org/2012/04/eight-healthy-coping-tips-to-manage-grief

Teamotions: www.teamotionstea.com

The Surprising Benefit of Going Through Hard Times
www.huffingtonpost.com/entry/post-traumatic-growth-creativity_us_568426c0e4b014efe0d9d8e8

The Truth About Post Traumatic Growth After Loss
www.whatsyourgrief.com/posttraumatic-growth-after-loss

Creatively Expressing Grief
www.journeyofhearts.org/kirstimd/create_grief.htm

Healing Artwork www.recover-from-grief.com/creativity-grief.html

Facets of Grief www.facetsofgrief.com


**Memorial Items**

Molly Bears www.mollybears.com

Comfort Cub www.thecomfortcub.com

National Star Registry www.starregistry.com

Seashore of Remembrance
www.theseashoreofremembrance.blogspot.com.au

Refuge in Grief Writing Course
www.refugeingrief.com/support/30-day

Illuminate Photography Course
www.berylaynyoung.com/illuminate

**Growing Your Family**

RESOLVE-Family Building Options

www.resolve.org/family-building-options

Still Mothers, Living Childless After Loss

www.stillmothers.com

Pregnancy After Loss

www.pregnancyafterlosssupport.com

CarlyMarie Project Heal, Pregnancy After Loss

www.carlymarieprojectheal.com/healing/pregnancy-after-loss

Postpartum Progress

www.postpartumprogress.com/having-a-baby-after-infant-loss-the-complicated-mix-of-grief-joy

# ABOUT THE AUTHOR

Amie Lands is a wife, mother, teacher and author. She is the proud founder of The Ruthie Lou Foundation and a Certified Grief Recovery Specialist®. Her most sacred role in life is being "mama" to 3 beautiful babes: her daughter Ruthie Lou, who she held for 33 days, and her two sons, Reid and Adam, whom, with her husband Chris, she is privileged to watch grow every day.

When Ruthie Lou died, Amie felt thrown into a sea of pain that she never wanted or imagined. She wandered the bookstores searching for a book that could help guide her through the unimaginable decisions she and her husband were facing and the lifetime of grief that they were embarking upon. She needed to know that others had survived this experience because she didn't believe that she could continue living with the pain of her broken heart.

Amie never found the exact book she was looking for. So, five years after the death of her daughter (and after finding that joy had crept back into her life), Amie wrote the words of her heart in honor of Ruthie Lou, to help other moms and dads in their journey of grief.

This is the book Amie searched for when her precious baby died.

Made in the USA
San Bernardino, CA
10 January 2020